GROUNDBREAKERS!

by Kevin and Val Moore

Scripture Union

//

Dedicated to James, Rebekah and Susanna, our three lovely children

With special thanks to the 1999 Overstrand Family Beach Mission team, children and young people who piloted and developed the programme.
Thanks to others in East Anglia and beyond who have sampled the material and contributed towards its creative development, especially Thetford Baptist Community Church.

Scripture Union, 207–209 Queensway, Bletchley, MK2 2EB, England.

© Kevin and Val Moore, 2001.

ISBN 1 85999 438 5

British Library Cataloguing-in-Publication Data
A catalogue record for this book is available from the British Library.

Cover illustration by Colin Smithson
Cover design by Grax Design
Internal design by Grax Design
Illustrations by Kevin Moore

Scripture quotations are from the Holy Bible, New International Version. Copyright © 1973, 1978, 1984 by International Bible Society. Anglicisation copyright © 1979, 1984, 1989. Used by permission of Hodder and Stoughton Limited.

Printed and bound by Ebenezer Baylis & Son Ltd.

//

Contents

Break new ground with Groundbreakers!	4
Creating the Construction Site (+ Site diagram)	5
Job descriptions and daily building schedule	6
Using Groundbreakers!	7
Using OHP and Video	9
Countdown to Groundbreakers!	10
Foremen's fillers and site games	11
Working with children and Team tactics	12
Stay legal!	13
Confidential declaration form	14
Sample registration letter and form	15
Consent form and publicity	16
Security and Registration	17
Groundbreakers! song	18
Groundbreakers! drama	19
Day One Late Man Jo	21
Day Two Walls Higher Nehemiah	29
Day Three Expert Engineer Elijah	37
Day Four Daring Designer Hezekiah	45
Day Five Jesus the Cornerstone	53
Groundbreakers! event for all ages	62
Parents and under-fives event; all-age service	63
Resources order form	64

Visit the 'GROUNDBREAKERS!' web site:

http://www.scriptureunion.org.uk/groundbreakers
The site includes song words and actions, prayer cards, competition sheets, artwork, fact files, drama scripts and bulletin board for ideas and comments.

Break new ground with Groundbreakers!

This material is designed to help you run a **GROUNDBREAKERS!** activity week or a short programme for a weekly or monthly children's club. It is full of ideas to help you work effectively with children with a wide variety of Bible experience, from none at all to a great deal!

- Are there children around who wouldn't naturally come into contact with the church?
- Do you feel a burden for families outside the church?
- Are you keen to develop your current children's ministry?
- Do you want to encourage and build up your existing children's team?
- Do you want your team of children's workers to discover and develop their gifts?
- Have you got time, energy and enthusiasm to reach out to others?

If the answer to any of the above is 'yes!', then **GROUNDBREAKERS!** could be for you!

GROUNDBREAKERS! runs on the theme of a construction site through which various Bible characters are introduced. God has broken into the lives of each of them and, in turn, they have gone out to break new ground for God. Each day, there is a drama about a more recent character who broke new ground with help from God. This demonstrates to the children that God has worked, not only through the lives of people in the Bible, but throughout history. He continues to do so today, even through the lives of the **GROUNDBREAKERS!** team.

This programme gives opportunities for small group work, creative activities, singing, interactive Bible stories, games, drama, competitions and the option of the **GROUNDBREAKERS!** video, all on the easily identifiable construction theme. It is laid out to be easily used over a five-day period, with additional suggestions for special events for parents and under-fives and all-ages. There are also ideas for how you could use **GROUNDBREAKERS!** over a three-day or eight-day programme. The material is not meant to be prescriptive in its layout but is flexible for you to adapt to your requirements.

When you decide to run **GROUNDBREAKERS!**, make sure you have clearly defined aims. Plan your follow-up strategy beforehand, to maintain the contacts you will have made with the children and families. Part of this strategy might be to set up a midweek **GROUNDBREAKERS!** club that nurtures the children on a weekly, fortnightly or monthly basis. You could also run **GROUNDBREAKERS!** family events at regular intervals throughout the year and give invitations for special all-age services.

Our desire is that **GROUNDBREAKERS!** provides you with a tool (pun intended!) to present and reveal the truth of the life-changing gospel message. Our prayer is that children and families will have the opportunity to respond to the Lord Jesus Christ and begin their journey of faith, or simply to take a step nearer to God. It could all begin at the Construction Site, where you lay the foundations through prayer, teaching, hard work and relationship-building with the children. Have fun!

Kevin and Val Moore

Thetford, UK
June 2000

Creating the Construction Site

Construction sites are a familiar sight all over the world. As you create your own Construction Site, make sure it suits your location and the space available. Use your imagination! The team are the Foremen, with a Site Manager. The children are the Builders, responsible to their Foremen divided into Site Corners (small groups).

Site Entrance: The main registration table. This can be sectioned-off with plastic defiance barriers, cones and flashing yellow safety lamps. To create a construction site environment, place some of the following around the registration area – a wheelbarrow, hard hat, spade, chipped tea mugs, muddy boots, opened packet of biscuits, a pile of rubble (made out of small bits of scrunched-up brown and orange paper). Erect construction signs at appropriate places around the building, such as: 'Men at Work'; 'Construction Site'; 'Hard Hat Area'; 'Restricted Access'; 'Pedestrians This Way'. These can be hired or made. Signs made out of fluorescent card can be positioned on doorways. The following signs are particularly helpful: 'Site Entrance', 'Site Exit', 'Site Manager's Office'. Cover these with self-adhesive transparent film for protection.

Site Manager's Office: This should be at the front of the main area. This can be a striped workman's hut or a table cordoned-off with defiance tape and flashing yellow lamps. The screen, visual presentation board, overhead projector and other electrical equipment should all be cordoned off with black and yellow electrical warning tape.

Site Corners: These can be spaced around the edge of the room, each having an orange cone, with some wall space and containing tables and chairs. Alternatively, you may try to create 'furniture' to be found on a construction site, such as boxes, crates and sacking. Watch out for sharp edges and splinters however!

Builders can be allocated to Site Corners according to age. Access to more than one room may mean that Site Corners could be in a venue other than in the Site Meeting Area.

Each Site Corner will be named after a piece of groundbreaking equipment, for example: Bulldozer; Digger; Front end loader; Concrete mixer; Truck; Crane. This name will be displayed on their Site Corner box which will contain their Builders' Bands, Digging sheets and any other bits. It keeps each Site Corner tidy!

Site Meeting Area: this needs to be a clear space in the centre, with cones marking the perimeter. Builders come together for the Site Meeting in this area.

Construction posters and photographs can be displayed on the walls.

Storage/Display Area: This could be by the Site Manager's Office, for hard hats, fluorescent jackets/vests, etc. The Site Manager can have a hard hat and fluorescent jacket/vest. If the budget allows, Foremen could also have fluorescent jackets/vests and different colour hard hats. Children can bring hard hats too if they have them. (These may be available from the Early Learning Centre or they can buy 'Bob the Builder' hats from toy shops.)

Cardboard scaffolding, taped together to form frames for displays, can be made out of lightweight tubes, eg poster tubes, kitchen rolls, protective foam pipe insulation. Teams will develop their Site Corners as the week progresses. Allow space for this.

A Site postbox can be made and positioned near the Site Manager's Office.

TIPS OF THE TRADE

A lot of equipment may be hired or purchased from your local tool hire firm or builder. Make enquiries about this early on in your planning!

Foremen's Yard: An area, preferably in another room, that is specifically for equipment and materials. Tables can be arranged for the display of all the art and craft resources. Boxes placed underneath the tables contain junk modelling items. The Foremen's Yard should be designated as 'Out of bounds' for the Builders.

Site Manager's Office (table area, etc.)

Easel & presentation area or TV & video player

OHP & Screen

Musicians

'GROUNDBREAKERS!' Postbox

SITE MEETING AREA

Site Entrance

Site Exit

Registration Area   Site Display

Job descriptions and building schedule

Site Manager: This is the person who is in charge and has overall responsibility for coordinating **GROUNDBREAKERS!**. He/she should wear a clip-on name badge, hard hat, **GROUNDBREAKERS!** or other T-shirt, preferably jeans or trousers and fluorescent jacket/vest.

Foremen: These are adult team members who are responsible for a group of children in their Site Corner. (Younger helpers are the Assistant Foremen.) They get to know the children as they work with them, assisting them in their activities, supervising and sharing with them. Some Foremen may double up as actors in the dramas or musicians. They can wear the same as the Site Manager except for a different colour hard hat (budget permitting). If you are running a large holiday club, you will need to appoint a Head Foreman to be team leader for each age group.

Surveyors: These are the registration and refreshment teams. They wear a clip-on name badge and have a different colour hard hat from the Foremen and Site Manager. If you have a smaller team, Surveyors can double up as Assistant Foremen.

Labourers: These are the general helpers, responsible for the behind the scenes setting up of equipment and other practical matters. They wear a clip-on name badge and the same colour hard hat as the Surveyors. If you have a smaller team, Labourers double up as Assistant Foremen.

Musicians and actors: Unless you have a large team, musicians and actors are also likely to be Foremen, Labourers or Surveyors.

CONSTRUCTION SITE PASSES SHOULD BE WORN BY ALL OF THE TEAM, SHOWING THAT THEY HAVE OFFICIAL SITE ACCESS.

Builders: These are the children who attend the programme. They can be encouraged to wear jeans or shorts and T-shirt or sweatshirt. Some children may like to wear their own hard hat if they have one. They should always wear a Builder's Band or Construction Site Pass for identification when on site (see page 17).

Construction terms are used for each section of the programme and will be used when talking to the children, to reinforce the theme. Develop other ideas yourself.

GROUNDBREAKERS! programme is written for primary children aged 4½ – 11 years of age. It assumes most groups will use the material for five days and for a two (or up to two-and-a-half) hour session. There are suggestions for a parents and under-fives event, best held during an afternoon, plus an all-age event and an all-age service for the final two days or as follow-up opportunities (see pages 62 and 63).

Daily Building Schedule

Site Corner preparations	30 minutes
Foremen's Fuel	25 minutes
Welcome	
Site Meeting	20 minutes
Digging /Activity sheets	30 minutes
Creative Construction	10–15 minutes
(including refreshments)	35 minutes
Site Clean-up	
Site Meeting	5 minutes
Foremen's Debrief	20 minutes
Construction Site Clear-up!	5–10 minutes
	30 minutes

The above programme is for approximately 2 hours. For a 2½ hour programme, increase the Creative Construction by 10 minutes, the Digging sheet time by 5 minutes, include a game (10 minutes) and include two more action songs or have a memory verse competition (5 minutes). For a 1½ hour programme, reduce the Creative Construction time by 10 minutes, reduce the first Site Meeting time by taking out one action song and the Reconstruction (saves 10 minutes), and take out the Building Presentations in the final Site Meeting (saves 10 minutes).

Using Groundbreakers!

Foremen's Fuel

This is not an optional extra! The Site Manager (and/or an appointed Foreman) coordinates the time of spiritual preparation for the team (Foremen's Fuel), before the Builders arrive. The aim is to get the focus right for the day (having already done the practical preparations for the session), committing everything to God in prayer. It is obviously essential that Foremen have already read the relevant Bible passages, as these will be integral to their preparations. The Foremen's Fuel offers a helpful outline rather than an in-depth study. Encourage participation from the group, keeping things moving and asking people to share succinctly. Try to include something from each section but don't worry if you can't cover every question. The Fact File gives brief information about the drama character of the day, serving as a helpful reminder as Builders may ask questions following the Reconstruction (drama). Fact Files can be made into acetates for use on the OHP if appropriate. Always ensure time for prayer.

Music

Background music quietly playing can be helpful as Builders arrive and during the Creative Construction. Some action songs are suggested for each session and music resource books. Abbreviations for sources for songs are as follows: SFK – *Songs of Fellowship for Kids*; S – *The Source*; KS –*Kidsource*; MP – *Mission Praise*; JP – *Junior Praise*; SH – *Spring Harvest Songbooks*; EP – *Everybody Praise*. Over the first two or three sessions the Groundbreakers! song can be gradually introduced (see page 18).

Site Corner starter

Children will need activities to do in the Site Corner when they first arrive. This is an important time for relationship building (see page 11 for ideas).

Bible stories

You may choose to use the **GROUNDBREAKERS!** video. This is a delightful and energetic account of the day's Bible **GROUNDBREAKERS!**, told in song by five puppets working on a building site. An alternative is to tell the Bible story yourself. If you choose to use the video rather than use the retold story (which goes into things in a little more detail), you will still need to read through the retold story yourself and check that the Builders have been given all of the information they need to fill in the Digging sheets.

A retold story outline is given at the end of each day's programme. These have been tried and tested and encourage interaction with the audience. These outlines are meant to be used as a basis for your talk, rather than as a word-for-word script so please adapt them for your situation. Builders are involved by answering questions, miming actions and positioning illustrations on the presentation board. Foremen should sit with the Builders and will also be involved in holding visuals, leading actions and encouraging the Builders to participate. You may find it useful to prime some Builders beforehand about actions and responses required. An appointed Foreman should be looking out for the first child to stand to attention in response to the title phrase. A storyteller needs to use simple, clear language, projecting the voice to the back of the room and not speaking too fast. It is advisable to practise the storytelling and use of visuals beforehand.

Reconstruction (drama)

Each Reconstruction stars recent historical characters who have all been groundbreaking pioneers, inspired by God. The final two Reconstructions give the opportunity for several children to be actors. Make sure you give them plenty of time to rehearse. All Reconstructions include interactive responses, which encourage the audience to concentrate on the content. They are true stories of the way God has broken new ground in the lives of people in the past 500 years. You will need to have a drama team to rehearse each one carefully, collecting and making the props as appropriate. The scripts are self-explanatory and are included in each day's programme.

Refreshments

Keep these simple. Check for allergies. It is recommended that each Site Corner goes for refreshments during Creative Construction, one group at a time.

Digging (activity) sheets

The Digging sheets use the New International Version of the Bible. Adapt them to the version of the Bible your church uses with children. The sheets reinforce the Bible teaching of the day and help the Builders learn the memory verse. They also give opportunities for Builders to ask questions and discuss the teaching. The sheets are to be used in the Digging time. It is a great opportunity for Foremen to build relationships with Builders. There are two sheets each day, one more suitable for under-eights, the other more suitable for Builders who are eight-plus. Choose what is right for each group.

Memory verses

These should be introduced during the main Site Meeting. Memory verses are important in encouraging Builders to learn verses from the Bible. This is all part of helping Builders to get to know God better. A very effective way of presenting the daily Memory verse is to build the verse as a display on the wall. It can be written on card-shaped stones or bricks using a different colour for each day's verse. Try removing bricks from any one verse to see if the Builders can remember it. By the end of the week can you remove them all?!

The Memory verse could also be written on an acetate and displayed on an OHP, where parts of the verse can be covered. Foremen and Builders are encouraged to learn the verses for the week. Builders try to catch the Foremen out! If a Builder can recite the verse but the Foreman cannot, the Builder could win a prize. The Site Manager recaps on the verse each day, during the final ten minutes. They will have been reinforced in the Site Corner Digging time.

Creative Construction (craft)

The importance of this activity is to give the Builders the opportunity to make something in two or three dimensions. This complements the Bible teaching and gives room for questions and discussion. These tried and tested activities will stimulate their learning together. The activity will enhance team work in the Site Corner and gives the Builders a chance to get to know each other and their Foremen. During the craft time, Foremen should be prepared to share any relevant personal stories or testimonies appropriate to their Site Corner Builders.

Prayer with Builders

When leading corporate prayer with children, take care to use simple, clear, modern English, keeping it brief and relevant. At the end of the session it would be appropriate to give thanks for the time spent together, for friendships made and things learnt.

Builders may well ask for prayer individually, or desire to respond to God by praying themselves. If a child asks for prayer, pray with them in the main hall, ideally in a designated quiet area (always in view of others). If you are unable to respond to such a request because it is in the middle of the Creative Construction or a key discussion with your Site Corner, assure the child they will have this opportunity shortly and when appropriate direct them to a Foreman in the prayer area, or to the Site Manager.

Prayer as a step of commitment

A child may indicate that they want to take a step to become a follower of Jesus. This may be for the first time or the tenth time. Ask the child if they have any questions and talk to them about the important step they are about to make. Explain clearly and simply what it means to ask Jesus to be their Lord, Saviour and friend and become his follower. Pray with them a simple prayer, pausing to allow them to repeat each phrase out loud. Alternatively read out a prepared prayer – see the booklets at the front of **GROUNDBREAKERS!**. Give them one of these booklets and show them how they can read more about what they have done. Tell them about the follow-up activities your church is running that are appropriate, eg midweek club, etc. A prayer card (see page 26) should be filled in for each child who responds, to show their parent after the session. It is helpful to find out if the child has access to a suitable children's Bible at home.

Games

The games are a minor part of the programme and are only to be used if weather, space and time permits. Simple games can be used as Builders arrive in their Site Corners, especially on the first two sessions. These should be short and aimed at getting to know the Builders. Games to encourage memory verse learning are invaluable. Quizzes on the Bible and drama characters of the week are also helpful and any games on the building theme should help cement the ideas! An optional short game prior to the finish of the session can be included. See page 11 for some game suggestions, and the **GROUNDBREAKERS!** web site.

TRIED AND TESTED
Setting up a game and organising it takes a deceptively long time! Previous planning is essential to be ready to roll.

Competition sheets

There are competition sheets on the web site which are designed for the Builders to take home and enter the daily competition. These are optional but fun and should be posted in the **GROUNDBREAKERS!** postbox in the site area at the next session. They often make the Builders more keen to come to the following session. Optional prizes can be given for the winners at the end of each session.

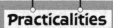

Using OHP and Video

Overhead projector presentation

An overhead projector is useful for words of songs, memory verses, activity and competition sheets, and gives additional options on storytelling. Small individual craft activities, such as the stained-glass window on Day 5, can be displayed on the screen. Visuals in this resource book can be enlarged and photocopied onto acetates.

- Always check you are using photocopiable acetates in the copier, as the wrong ones will damage your machine.

- Downloading from the **GROUNDBREAKERS!** web site will give complementary resource material to put onto acetates for display purposes. A computer shop, print copy facility, or design studio will (for a charge) download onto disk for you to adapt.

- Artwork can be reduced or enlarged using the photocopier and cut and pasted into a new format before photocopying onto acetate. A graphic designer would be able to do this or a local print copy facility.

- A design print studio will be able to make up colour acetates for the OHP, colour transparencies for slide projectors, A2 or A1 posters for the noticeboard, visual aids for the presentations, etc.

- Word acetates for songs and memory verses are best printed using black type in a clear, bold, lowercase, sans serif (without the curly bits) font. Colour-blind people will not see coloured lettering very well.

- Make sure your acetates are of a consistent size and format, landscape (horizontal) or portrait (vertical). These can be framed with a cardboard mount (useful for having notes on when speaking) or a cardboard frame taped to the OHP screen to make a fixed mount.

- Always keep spare OHP bulbs and fuses. A floor mat to cover the electrical cable is sensible, when working with children, to avoid tripping.

Video presentation

The **GROUNDBREAKERS!** video contains an imaginative retelling of the story of each day's Bible character who broke new ground for God. The video is an investment as it is a reusable resource in your continuing teaching programme and as a helpful follow-up to **GROUNDBREAKERS!**. The video, of course, is only one way of presenting the Bible stories, which is why a story outline is also provided in this programme. You will have to decide what best suits your group and gifts within the team. Foremen should sit with their Builders when they watch the video, to maintain quiet order and to enable good discussion in their Site Corners later on. Children rarely share their television experience alongside adults.

Setting up a VCR and TV (with additional TV sets for larger groups) is not technically difficult. Ask someone in your church to look into this so that Labourers know how to set it up. The visual and sound quality are the most important elements of the video presentation, in order to hold your audience's attention. A sound system with the audio signal from the VCR directed through it, works better for larger groups particularly in large rooms. Sound amplification for smaller groups is always preferable if possible. The larger the screen the better, so you may like to explore possibilities. You may have someone in your church or area who has expertise in setting up a creative presentation with more than one TV screen. If all else fails, your local TV rental shop should be able to advise and supply you with the necessary equipment.

Video projectors may be available to hire or borrow from schools, organisations, or churches. You will need to be able to blackout the room or hall. Handle the equipment and bulbs carefully. They are expensive!

TIPS OF THE TRADE

Check each day, that the equipment and blackout is working properly, the sound is of good quality, the seating is arranged for optimum visibility, the video is lined up at the right point and light is not reflecting on the screen to impair visibility.

Presentation board

A large presentation board, covered in loop nylon (blue if available) is suggested for the storytelling. This will hold the fish, bricks, altar, tunnel and archway visuals in place if they have hook 'Velcro' on the back. Loop nylon is obtainable in self-adhesive rolls. Fluted plastic makes a very effective lightweight board when covered with loop nylon. Place the board on an easel or stand.

TIPS OF THE TRADE

Check that you have the right acetates for the day, all the equipment is working properly and that screen is set up for good visibility.

Countdown to Groundbreakers!

Allow a minimum of six months' planning to ensure you put on a stimulating and well-prepared programme. You will need a team of committed people who will take on various roles and responsibilities. This should all be underpinned by prayer from the rest of the church. Delegate jobs, wherever possible, according to people's gifts.

12 months to go

- Meet to prayerfully discuss and agree that to run **GROUNDBREAKERS!** is the right course of action to enable effective outreach to children and families.

- Plan a **GROUNDBREAKERS!** financial budget, including funds for follow-up (such as the creation of midweek groups and special events).

- Decide precise dates and book the venue.

- Encourage people to book in on First Aid/Basic Food Hygiene courses (as appropriate).

6 months to go

- Purchase copies of the **GROUNDBREAKERS!** book and video.

- Plan monthly meeting dates in the diary, with two training sessions in the final month.

- Check that the venue is safe and suitable and will offer the right space for the programme.

5 months to go

- Consult the introduction pages in the **GROUNDBREAKERS!** book and look at the practical bits of the programme.

- Discuss the maximum number of children you can safely accommodate (see page 13) and decide on the size of team needed.

- Discuss the various job responsibilities, appoint team members to be responsible for various tasks and recruit new team.

4 months to go

- Discuss the publicity (including quantities required) and how you will advertise and invite the children and families. The Publicity Coordinator can now produce literature (see pages 15 and 16).

- Arrange dates to visit the local schools.

- Start collecting junk modelling equipment, construction pictures, etc.

- Ensure you have people responsible for all the jobs (see page 6).

- Musicians begin to practise the **GROUNDBREAKERS!** song.

- Plan dramas and retold Bible storytelling.

- Plan your follow-up events in the diary.

3 months to go

- Discuss the activities and give equipment needs to the Resources Coordinator.

- Ask the Art/Design Coordinator to prepare work on the stories for days 1 and 2.

- Approach the local tool hire firm for equipment.

- Review your follow-up strategy.

- Ask the General Helps Coordinator to make the site postbox.

- Distribute team application forms.

- Information Coordinator to let the Social Services know that you are planning a special week. (See page 13 for legal implications.)

- Discuss your child protection policy and appropriate course of action to cover incidents and accidents.

2 months to go:

- Ask the Art/Design Coordinator to prepare work on the stories for days 3 to 5. Look at Days 1 and 2 and decide how to present the story involving several people.

- Incorporate the songs you will be using, in the church services before **GROUNDBREAKERS!**

- Discuss the practical details of the parents and under-fives event, all-age event and all-age service.

- Review publicity. Publicity Coordinator advises on distribution strategy, including school visits and poster sites.

- Order T-shirts/resources from CPO (see page 64 and inside back cover), make your fluorescent arm bands (see page 17). Order follow-up literature and Bible reading notes for children (see inside front cover).

- Ask team to write to people who would pray for them during **GROUNDBREAKERS!**

- Explore the soft play equipment for the parents and under-fives event.
- Site Manager prepares the morning team briefs.
- View the **GROUNDBREAKERS!** video.
- Rehearse **GROUNDBREAKERS!** special drama and distribute scripts for Reconstructions.
- Display and distribute publicity.

1 month to go

- Look at the retold Bible stories for days 3 to 5 and decide how to present the story involving several people.
- Arrange to pick up construction equipment.
- Finish making props, collect Site Corner boxes, photocopy activity/competition sheets.
- Check registration and refreshment teams are prepared, and the catering for the family event is organised.
- Arrange hire of video/TV equipment (if using).

One week to go

The final training session should ideally be held in the **GROUNDBREAKERS!** venue. This should be compulsory for all involved and works well as a time of prayer and preparation for the team. Some churches arrange this for a Sunday afternoon followed by a commissioning service for the whole team. The following areas should all be covered:

- Aims and objectives of the whole programme.
- Site Manager to go through Day 1 and the timing of the day's programme in detail and practicalities such as registration, retelling the Bible story, showing the video, music, dramas, refreshments, activities, presentations and using the construction site venue.
- Recap on tasks, responsibilities and people involved.
- Recap on memory verses and how they are used.
- Discuss the way to pray with children and use of appropriate literature plus working with children (see pages 8 and 12).
- Rehearse some of the action songs.
- Allow time for prayer and fine tuning.

The day before Groundbreakers! starts:

Set up as much equipment as you can, prepare the Construction Site. Each day, electrical equipment should be tested beforehand and set up an hour or so before the programme begins (see page 9).

Foremen's fillers

The following games and activities are fillers for Foremen to use, in their Site Corners, at appropriate gaps in the **GROUNDBREAKERS!** programme:

1 Play a game of catch with a Builder's glove, using each Builder's name.
2 Make up your own Site Corner song, shout or response on the construction theme (perhaps with some actions too!).
3 Find out about each other's hobbies and interests. Ask everyone to sketch them on a piece of paper.
4 Play 'Twenty Questions' based on the construction theme. Builders guess the item chosen, using up to twenty questions, with yes or no answers only.
5 Invent a tongue-twister on the construction theme!
6 Write down a question for Site Manager to answer, or a construction joke, and post in the postbox.
7 Discuss your favourite fillings for Builders' sandwiches and invent names to call them.

Site games

1 Construction Sites: Based on 'Traffic Lights' where instructions are called out and Builders have to respond accordingly. The last Builder to respond (or any who get it wrong) are out. The instructions are:

'Scaffolding': *Stretch up as tall as you can on tiptoe.*
'Earth': *Curl up in a ball on the ground.*
'Pneumatic drill': *Jump on the spot as fast as you can.*
'Cement mixer': *Turn round and round on the spot.*
'Tea break': *Sit with crossed legs, holding an imaginary cuppa.*
'Digger': *Walk around with arms held in front, with hands cupped in a scoop shape.*
'White lining': *Stand on one leg and swing the other.*
'Clock off': *Everyone freezes on the spot.*

2 Foreman says...: As per 'Simon Says...' but on a construction theme. Use the ideas above, and your own.

3 Builders' stations: Everyone is allocated an object/ vehicle found on a construction site and sits on a chair in a circle (no vacant chairs). One Builder, stands in the middle. A Foreman calls out the names of several objects and these Builders/Foremen have to change places. The one who doesn't find a vacant chair is then in the middle.

4 Builders' quiz: Make up a quiz with questions on the various memory verses, Bible characters, etc, of the sessions. As Builders answer correctly they receive a cone. When all the cones are used up, the Site Corner with the most cones is the winner.

Working with children and Team tactics

Working with children

Being aware of children and the world in which they live is very important when getting to know them and sharing yourself with them. Here are some helpful tips:

- Go down to their level and eye level whenever possible. Try to see things as they see them.

- Learn their names early on.

- Listen to them. Don't do all the talking.

- Take an interest in their hobbies and interests. Ask about their schools, heroes, favourite TV shows.

- Involve all the children in the team and delegate tasks.

- Look for opportunities to affirm and encourage. Reward success without highlighting failure.

- Know what is happening in the next part of the programme. Be prepared with various gap fillers for those spare moments.

- Sit with the children rather than standing around the edges of the room. Direct the focus of their attention to the front when items are going on.

- Diffuse disturbances calmly, separate disruptive children when practical, or sit next to or between them.

- Define the boundaries, eg Don't leave the building or wander off, run, or touch the electrical equipment!

- Build up expectations, build in surprises.

- Be patient and prayerful.

- Be sensitive to any special needs.

- Enthusiastically join in with all the programme, learn the actions for the songs, learn the memory verses.

- Show you have a sense of humour.

- Be up to date on any national/local news stories that may be conversation openers.

- Use language children will understand, not Christian jargon or long words which will result in a loss of concentration.

- Many children today do not go to church and are unfamiliar with the Bible. Many children will be keen to learn spiritual truths from the Bible.

- Vary your voice tone and don't shout.

- Don't have favourites.

- Don't make promises you don't intend to keep.

- Don't be tactile with children, nor allow yourself to be in a room on your own with them. Always talk and pray with children where you can be clearly seen. Sadly, touching children is not advisable now, although the government have recently made it clear that such actions as guiding with a hand on the shoulder or comforting a distressed child would not be considered inappropriate.

- Be ready to share how God has answered prayer in your life in a clear and brief manner.

- Be aware at the end of the week that it is not so much what you have said and done, but how you have done it, that will be remembered.

Team tactics

Running a special week requires good team work. The following are some helpful tips:

- Remember you are working with others, not on your own. You can learn from others and they can learn from you.

- Look to encourage other team members who may get tired in the course of the week. Be aware of less experienced team members, or those who may be personally finding life difficult.

- Pray for the other team members, for health, encouragements and answers to prayer.

- If you are ever unsure of what you are to do or you need assistance, ask for help from the Site Manager or another Foreman. Never leave your team alone, but send your Assistant Foreman with a message.

- Think through the items you will need each day, write a list and compile your equipment the day/evening before.

- Read through the Bible passage again the night before, revise the memory verse, pray for wisdom and guidance in the way you work and speak with the children, pray for good sleep for all involved.

- Be a good timekeeper, respond to the time announcements during the craft/activity time.

- Enjoy the **GROUNDBREAKERS!** experience and pray that God will do in and through you all he desires.

Stay Legal!

The welfare of the children we hope to reach through **GROUNDBREAKERS!** is of paramount importance. We are not only concerned for their spiritual welfare, but also for their physical and emotional welfare. Sadly nowadays, children are at risk as much as ever before, and it is our duty to do all we can to ensure their safety and well-being as we aim to show them God's love.

All team members should be made aware of the current legislation on issues to do with daycare of children, especially relating to children under eight years old. But they are appropriate for all children attending a church-run event. The following details are correct at the time of going to print. But you are advised to check with your local Social Services and the Churches' Child Protection Advisory Service (contact details below) nearer the time of your **GROUNDBREAKERS!** programme.

- You may need to register **GROUNDBREAKERS!** with Social Services if you use your premises for more than two hours in a day. As long as you meet for less than six days in any one year, no registration is required. If under-eights are present, you should inform Social Services in writing of your plans. However, it is good practice to advise them whatever your plans. Any holiday club/activity week over two hours, which runs for more than six days in a year, must be registered. So if you are planning follow-up events, it is likely to affect you. If in doubt phone Social Services and check with the Local Day Care Advisor – he/she is there to help! Each local Social Services will have different procedures and recommendations so check what is considered good practice in your area.

Even if you don't need to register, give careful consideration to the following requirements laid down by the Children Act as sensible guidelines to be interpreted with common sense.

- Requirements for accommodation state that the premises should be warm, clean and adequately lit and ventilated, with clearly marked emergency exits.

- Minimum unencumbered floor space to be provided for children aged 5–8 years is 25 square feet (2.3 square metres) per child so be careful about large numbers of children in a small hall. Work out the maximum number of children who can attend.

- The premises you use should meet the Health and Safety requirements. Check that the owners of the premises have complied with all the requirements.

Ideally there should be one toilet and one hand basin for every ten children. If you are preparing food on site, you will need to be inspected by the Environmental Health Officer. The person with overall responsibility for the catering arrangements should have the minimum of the Basic Food and Hygiene Certificate. Smoking should not be permitted on the premises. Children should not be allowed unsupervised access to the kitchen.

- Any accidents or incidents occurring during a session must be recorded in an Accident/Incident Book. This is essential in the event of any insurance claim. A record of the matter should be noted, along with any details of the action taken. It should be countersigned where appropriate.

- Everyone should be made aware of emergency procedures and fire exits. There must be access to a telephone. At least one first-aid kit must be easily accessible and at least one **GROUNDBREAKERS!** team member should have a working knowledge of first aid with an accompanying up-to-date certificate.

- All groups must have the appropriate liability insurance. Make sure your activity is adequately covered by the policy of your church or organisation.

- Proper procedures should be in place for appointing team members, including the completion of a team member application form, and provision of at least one reference. This is now good practice amongst many churches, to better cover all team members under the church's liability insurance policy, to screen suitable team and to better safeguard children.

- Recommendations for adult to child ratios are as follows:
  - For 0–2 years – 1 adult to every 3 children (1:3)
  - For 2–3 years – 1 adult to every 4 children (1:4)
  - For 3–8 years – 1 adult to every 8 children (1:8)
  - For over eights – 1 adult for the first 8 children (1:8), followed by 1 for every 12 (1:12).

There should always be more than one adult for any group and one should be female.

- You must have an agreed child protection procedure in the case of a child alleging or disclosing abuse or a situation which puts them at risk. (If you need advice contact the Churches' Child Protection Advisory Service on 01322 667207/660011, e-mail info@ccpas.co.uk or see web site at www.ccpas.co.uk)

Confidential declaration form for potential team members

(This is the requirement for use in the UK. If using **GROUNDBREAKERS!** in other parts of the world, check current legislation and what is required.) For further information or advice in the UK, contact the Churches' Child Protection Advisory Service.

Most denominations now have established good practice policies. All churches, whether denominational or not, should have clear child protection policies. Where such good practice is ignored insurance may be invalid. If you have an established procedure for your church, all of the holiday club team must go through the process. If you have not, a special activity week like **GROUNDBREAKERS!** will provide a good opportunity and incentive to develop one. The following notes outline the main issues.

All employed people with access to children (that is, anyone under the age of eighteen) have, by law, to make a signed declaration of any criminal record. A key recommendation in *Safe From Harm* (HMSO) also requires such a statement from volunteers. Failure to take the necessary steps could lead to a claim of negligence against the church, if a child comes to any harm at the hand of anyone working with them in a voluntary capacity. 'Harm' includes ill-treatment of any kind (including sexual abuse), or impairment of physical or mental health or development, or neglect.

You should ask all potential team members to sign a form such as the one below.

CONFIDENTIAL DECLARATION

- When using such a form, emphasise that it represents positive action for good practice, and slur or suspicion is not implied. Obviously the nature of the form is sensitive and should be handled confidentially.

- Ensure that confidentiality is maintained. In accordance with the Data Protection Act, do not divulge any information to third parties.

- If anyone gives a 'yes' answer, allow the individual to explain this disclosure personally or by letter. If you are in any doubt about the person's suitability, consult your church leader.

- As well as the declaration form, it is recommended that potential team members offer one or more names as a referee.

A referee needs to know that the team member will be working with children and young people. Questions to them might include:

In what capacity have you known the applicant, and for how long?

How willing and able is he/she to work with others?

How suitable would you consider him/her for work with children and young people?

Are there any relevant details about this applicant which cause you concern?

CONFIDENTIAL DECLARATION

Guidelines from the Home Office following the Children Act 1989 require that all voluntary organisations, including churches, take steps to safeguard the children who are entrusted to their care. You are therefore asked to make the following declarations:

Do you have any current or spent criminal convictions, cautions, bindovers or cases pending?   Yes ☐   No ☐

Have you ever been held liable by a court for a civil wrong, or had an order made against you by a matrimonial or a family court? Yes ☐   No ☐

Has your conduct ever caused, or been likely to cause harm to a child or put a child at risk, or, to your knowledge, has it ever been alleged that your conduct has resulted in any of these things?   Yes ☐   No ☐

Signed .... Date ....

Because of the nature of the work for which you are applying, this post is exempt from the provision of Section 4 (ii) of the Rehabilitation of Offenders Act 1974, by virtue of the Rehabilitation of Offenders Act 1974 (Exemptions) Order 1975, and you are therefore not entitled to withhold information about convictions which, for other purposes are 'spent' under the provisions of the Act. In the event of an appointment, any failure to disclose such convictions could result in the withdrawal of approval to work with children in the church.

Sample registration letter and form

Relevant name, address, logo for church/organisation
Contact phone number
Date

Dear Parent/Adult with parental responsibility,

This is an opportunity for your child to become a Builder for the week from (*day and date*) to (*day and date*), on the Construction Site at (*venue*), as part of the exciting **GROUNDBREAKERS!** programme run by (*church/organisation*). The week will provide a fun, informative and action-packed programme of events.

GROUNDBREAKERS! is suitable for primary school children aged 4$\frac{1}{2}$ to 11 years (*whatever your target age*). The Construction Site will be open to the Builders daily from (*time*) to (*time*). Access for Builders is free of charge (*or state cost to Builders*).

The Construction Site will be open for other special events as advertised (*eg parents and under-fives and all-age events*).

We look forward to recruiting some enthusiastic Builders. If you would like your child to be included in **GROUNDBREAKERS!**, please complete and return the enclosed form by (*date*). There is a limit to the number of Builders who can be on the Construction Site, for safety reasons, so please book in early to avoid disappointment. The (*church/organisation*) will confirm that your Builder has been registered. We look forward to building with your child at **GROUNDBREAKERS!**.

Your Name

Site Manager of **GROUNDBREAKERS!**

Registration form for GROUNDBREAKERS! (*Allow enough space for details*.)

Please cut along the dotted line and return to the Site Manager at (*church/organisation*) (One form per child please.)

Full name of child .... M/F   Date of birth ....

Address ....

.... Postcode ....

Telephone number .... Parent's mobile telephone number ....

School .... Age on first day of **GROUNDBREAKERS!** ....

Contact number(s) during **GROUNDBREAKERS!** ....

Relevant information we should know: ....

....

Signature of parent/adult with parental responsibility ....

Name (printed) ....

The value of registration before the event is that you can know fairly accurately who is coming, so you can prepare well and are not likely to break any safety regulations. It also encourages commitment. However, it does mean some children may end up on a waiting list and may feel excluded.

Consent Form and publicity

///

(It is essential for this form to be completed, one for each child, in order that they may participate in the **GROUNDBREAKERS!** programme. It might also be worth checking with your local Social Services team whether there is any other information they recommend that you request.)

Please complete and return to the **GROUNDBREAKERS!** registration team.

Full name of child .... M/F .... Date of birth ....

Address ....

.... Postcode ....

Telephone number .... Parent's mobile number ....

Emergency contact number(s) during **GROUNDBREAKERS!** ....

I authorise only .... to collect my child

GP's name and telephone number ....

Relevant information we should know (eg allergies, behavioural difficulties, special needs, etc)

....

....

In the unlikely event of illness or accident I give my permission for any appropriate first aid treatment to be given by the nominated first aider. In an emergency, and if I cannot be contacted, I give consent for my child to receive treatment by a GP and/or hospital, including treatment under general anaesthetic. I understand that every effort will be made to contact me as soon as possible.

I confirm that the above details are correct to the best of my knowledge.

Signature of parent/adult with parental responsibility ....

Name (printed) ....

Publicity

Good, well-produced publicity, with accurate information, will be important when communicating with children and their families about the **GROUNDBREAKERS!** events. Design your publicity to be informative and attractive to those you want to reach. You might like to consider the following suggestions:

- Appoint a Publicity Coordinator whose work begins six months before **GROUNDBREAKERS!**.

- An A4 leaflet, folded twice and made into a concertina with the details of the programme works well (ideal to give to children and families). This may include an advance booking form, sample letter, or the Registration Form (see page 15) alongside your other attractive publicity (eg printing your programme details on the A5 CPO leaflet (see inside back cover). Work out quantities of publicity required to cover the local schools, children's groups, playgroups, etc with whom you have links. Decide when these letters should go out.

- The local school (or schools) will be a key place to arrange for publicity to be given out. Advance booking forms or Registration forms can be returned, if appropriate, via the school office/postbox, or to your church postbox.

- A4 and A2 posters can be produced (see CPO blank posters) and placed in strategic positions such as noticeboards in the local library, newsagents, etc. For outdoor use, the A4 posters can be laminated for protection.

- The Publicity Coordinator can produce an article with a good photograph for the local newspaper before and after the event(s).

- Publicity flyers can be produced for the parents and under-fives, all-age and follow-up events.

- The publicity should go out at least three to four weeks beforehand.

- You need good publicity to ensure that the event is well known. However, remember that it may also attract the attention of those with a less than healthy interest in young children, so be vigilant.

Security and Registration

The **GROUNDBREAKERS!** Construction Site will need to be a safe and secure environment for the Foremen and Builders to participate effectively. Having an efficient registration system in place is most important for the smooth running of the programme and for the protection of everyone, the site equipment and craft items made during the week.

Advance registration

Use appropriately designed Registration Forms (see page 15). This should enable a good percentage of the Builders to pre-book. Builders can then be allocated to the appropriate Site Corners depending on age. Site Corner areas (see page 5) should be designed for children in specific age groups.

As children enter, they register at the Site Entrance. The main Registration Area should hold names of those already booked and allocated to Site Corners. New children also need to be registered and allocated. All parents/adults with parental responsibility must complete a Consent Form for each child, with important information. This should be held at the main Registration Area. Children should be escorted to their Site Corners and introduced to their Foreman. This is especially important on the first day.

If older children arrive on their own, check that their parents know they have come and give them a Consent Form at the end of the first session, for parents to return, at the next session, to the main Registration Area.

Each child is given a Builder's Band in their Site Corner on which they write their name. Alternatively you could give each child a Construction Site Pass (see below). Special needs information will have already been given to the Foreman for those who have pre-booked. Such information

for all children registering on the day must also be passed to the Foreman.

The Foreman in charge of the Site Corner should keep registration details of Builders attending each session. This is essential in the event of an emergency evacuation of the building.

A master list of all those attending should be held by the Registration Team and updated each session. Ideally this should be on computer and include special needs requirements, emergency contact number(s), person(s) responsible to collect, etc. This is confidential information.

Each Site Corner ideally will have two or three Foremen (or Assistant Foremen), one being female, and not more than eight Builders to each Foreman.

Departure

For security reasons each Builder should give their Builder's Band to their Foreman before leaving the building.

Ideally parents/adults with parental responsibility should come through one well-signed entrance and leave the building through another exit. This should prevent a bottleneck of people in the entrance area and allow Foremen to chat to collectors as they come through the Site area. For maximum security, children should return to their Site Corner to be collected from there.

At the start of the week, parents/adults with parental responsibility should be issued with five different numbered/coloured Site Corner Passes to hand in to the Site Corner Foreman as they collect their child each day.

Construction Site Pass

Name:

GROUNDBREAKERS!
APPROVED

Official Construction Site Access

Construction Site Pass: available from CPO (see inside back cover), or you can make them by photocopying onto light coloured card and inserting into a plastic name-tag holder. Alternatively, you can design your own badges.

SUGGESTED BUILDERS' BAND

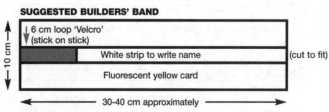

To prepare Builders' bands: cut various lengths (eg 30-40 cm of fluorescent yellow card, 10 cm wide). Attach 6 cm of stick on stick loop 'Velcro' centrally on left-hand end (as above) and a white strip of paper running the rest of the length of the card. Have 6 cm strips of stick on stick hook 'Velcro' ready.

To assemble Band: measure band around child's upper arm with a 6 cm overlap. Remove band and cut off excess card, allowing for the 6 cm overlap. Stick a hook 'Velcro' 6 cm strip inside, on the opposite end to the loop 'Velcro', to fasten. Write name on the band and fit to Builder!

Groundbreakers!

Val Moore
arranged by G.E. Hutchinson

Groundbreakers! Song

Introduction: Musicians play the last two lines of the chorus.

Chorus: (with 'life')
Jesus is around now,
Still breaking new ground, wow!
Yes, Jesus is around.
And the sound that's around is of breaking new ground,
And the sound that's around is of breaking new ground!

Our ground is often hard when we hear your word.
Do we want to let you break in?
Do we want to let you break in?

Chorus: Jesus is around now...

When our ground's broken up, your Holy Spirit builds.
Holy Spirit, won't you come in?
Holy Spirit, won't you come in?

Chorus: Jesus is around now...

Without the cross we wouldn't have a part to play;
Lord, we want to serve you today,
Lord, we want to serve you today.

Chorus: Jesus is around now…

May we be your tools to help you break more ground?
Use us if you can, in this way,
Use us if you can, in this way.

Chorus: Jesus is around now...

Musicians play last two lines of chorus. Everyone stamps their feet and shouts together: '**GROUNDBREAKERS!**'

© Val Moore, 1999

Actions for 'GROUNDBREAKERS!' chorus:

Jesus - *point up high with right arm and forefinger.*
is around now, - *draw a large circle in front of you, with right forefinger.*
Still breaking - *clenched fists and act as if snapping a branch.*
new ground, wow! - *right foot, left foot stamp.*
Yes, Jesus - *point up high with right arm and forefinger.*
is around. - *draw a large circle in front of you, with right forefinger.*
And the sound - *cup right hand to right ear.*
that's around - *draw a large circle in front of you, with right forefinger.*
is of breaking - *clench fists and act as if snapping a branch.*
new ground! - *right foot, left foot stamp.*

Repeat last line.

(At the end of last chorus only)
Groundbreakers! - *repeated stamping whilst shouting Groundbreakers!!*

Groundbreakers! Drama

Use this drama at the all-age event and service, and to publicise the Groundbreakers! week. If you have time why not use it on Day 1 too!

Characters: *Team member; Pneum Atic; Shov All; I Pickit; J C Bdigger.*

Props: *Team member wears ordinary clothes and carries a clipboard (for script if needed); toolmen all wear scruffy trousers and T-shirt, fluorescent jacket/ vest (optional), gloves (optional) and hard hat (except for Pneum); Pneum has a pneumatic drill (cardboard) and ear protectors (real); Shov All carries a spade (large toy or cardboard); I Pickit has a pick (cardboard); J C Bdigger holds a steering wheel (real/toy/ cardboard) and tube exhaust (cardboard) on shoulders.*

TIPS OF THE TRADE

Your local car breakers may let you have an old steering wheel very cheaply. Fluorescent cycle vests are cheaper than jackets, ask around to see if anyone has one already. Workman's gloves, ear protectors, hard hats, etc can be purchased from a local tool hire firm.

Characters are off-stage, at different locations in the audience (except for JCB who is out of the room). Pneum needs to be in the middle of the audience; Shov at the side near the front; Pick on the other side and JCB drives in from the back.

The team member is at the front, about to say/do something but is interrupted by the noise of a pneumatic drill in the audience, as Pneum stands, acting out using his pneumatic drill, making as loud a noise as possible.

TIPS OF THE TRADE

A team member with the full script can prompt if necessary.
Toolmen shouldn't stand in a neat row at the front, but do make sure they face the audience.

TRIED AND TESTED
Make life-size tools from cardboard and stick script on the back.

Team member: Excuse me! Could you please sit down. (*No response from Pneum.*) Prod him someone, will you! (*Someone prods him.*)

Pneum: (*Jumps and looks up, surprised. Removes ear protectors.*) It is very dangerous to make me jump when I am using this drill! (*Shows it to the audience*)

Team member: Sorry, but who are you and what do you think you are doing?

Pneum: My name is Pneum; Pneum Atic and I am preparing the ground to build a motorway.

Team member: A motorway?! No way! Not here! There are no plans for a motorway to come through this construction site!

Pneum: Oh yes, mate. That's why I'm 'breaking new ground', just about, er... (*moves to the front*) here. (*Puts on ear protectors and prepares to start drilling.*)

Shov: (*Stands up gesturing with arms and shovel*) Now, can we just shove all you lot over there? I need to start 'breaking new ground' just about... here. (*He comes to the front, to one side.*)

Team member: And just who might you be?

Shov: I'm Shov; Shov All.

Team member: Well you can't just shove all of us about, you know. What do you think you are doing?

Shov: Motorway building; the ground needs breaking up first, you know.

Team member: So we've heard. But this is a totally unsuitable site.

TIPS OF THE TRADE

Speak slowly and clearly so the audience don't miss the puns.

Pickit: (*Interrupts with his pick*) With all of you sitting here it does look that way. I don't know quite how I'm going to pick (*makes his way to the front but not near the others*) my way through!

Team member: Not another one! And who might you be?

Pickit: My name's Pickit; I Pickit.

Team member: And don't tell me you are picking a spot here for breaking up the ground for a new motorway?

Pickit: That's right. I may not have picked the best moment, but I'm going to take up my pick and bring it down to 'break new ground'. (*He swings his pick.*)

Team member: I can't think why anyone would want a motorway here, anyway! Why don't you all go away now and only come back when you have some, er, written permission.

JCB: (*Driving in, making an exaggerated 'brumming' noise*) Who said we need permission? I've been 'breaking new ground' all my life and I don't know anything about permission.

Team member: (*Showing impatience*) Dare I ask your name?

JCB: Bdigger; J C Bdigger and I've got work to do! (*Revs up and drives around showing his manoeuvring skills as he comes to the front.*)

Team member: Now let's get this straight... (*gesturing with arm*)

All Toolmen: (*In unison*) At last; that's what we are trying to do...

Team member: I mean you can't build a motorway here! And what is the point of breaking up the ground first anyway?

Shov: (*Scratching head with shovel*) I dunno.

Pickit: (*Beginning to clean finger nails with pick*) We can't pick and choose you know.

Pneum: It's what my drill was made for (*scratching his back with drill*).

JCB: It might not be important for them to know why they are 'breaking new ground' but, being as important as I am, I can answer your question...

Others: (*In unison*) Oh yeah!?!

JCB: To make a strong and lasting road, the ground has to be broken up first and levelled. Then the various layers of the road structure are layered until it is ready to be surfaced and used. The road needs a good foundation and needs to be laid in the right place...

Team member: (*Interrupting*) In the right place; just my point! (*Pause, toolmen all looking expectantly at team member.*) But what you said is interesting because it is something like our lives. (*Pause.*) If we want to follow Jesus – that is go in the right direction and have Jesus as the best foundation – some things in our lives have got to be broken up first.

Others: (*Looking completely baffled*) Er? (*Scratch heads with respective tools.*)

Team member: The wrong things we say and do have to be broken up so that we are ready to change and the Holy Spirit can start building in us and with us.

Pickit: I can't quite pick it up but, come on JC, let's go and find out about permission. (*Turns to leave.*)

JCB: All right, let's go and find this written permission. Come on everyone!

Pneum: If you insist.

Shov: Are you giving us the shove, love?!

Team member: You could say that! (*All exit, noisily.*)

TIPS OF THE TRADE

When children call out the 'Groundbreakers!' response, be ready to repeat the sentence if necessary.

LATE MAN JO!

BLUEPRINT REFERENCE

JONAH: 1–4

Memory Verse   '**Jonah obeyed the word of the Lord and went to Nineveh.'**

Jonah 3:3a (*See Using* **GROUNDBREAKERS!**, *page 8*.)

AIMS

* To understand that *God* can use people like Jonah (in spite of faults they may have) to take *God's* message to others.

* To realise that the people of Nineveh may not have known how badly they were behaving until Jonah gave them *God's* message. When they heard Jonah, they said sorry to *God* and changed their behaviour.

* To understand that when Jonah changed his mind and did the right thing, *God* was able to use him.

* To realise that *God* can use all people, including children, if they are willing.

* To know that, because we make mistakes, we need to say sorry to *God* and then to do the things he wants.

the plumb line

What is sin?

We are naturally disobedient to God, whether we know him or not. It is not just the wrong things we say, do and think, but our fallen human nature which separates us from the Holy God. 'For all have sinned and fall short of the glory of God, and are justified freely by his grace through the redemption that came by Christ Jesus' (Romans 3:23,24).

Preparing Construction Site: Check that the Construction Site is set out correctly for the session. (*For general instructions and ideas, see page 5*.)

Foremen's Fuel (25 minutes)

(*See Using* **GROUNDBREAKERS!**, *page 7*.)

The Bible is God's word to humanity. It is powerful and life-changing. Jonah, and John Wesley (today's central drama character), in spite of their weaknesses, boldly shared God's word to other people and lives were changed. As a groundbreaking team, you will be sharing

and relating God's powerful Word to children. Pray, as a team, that God will powerfully speak into the lives of the children through all that you do today.

Open with a short prayer.

Bible reading: Jonah chapters 1–3 (select parts of these chapters).

Questions for the Site Manager to put to the Foremen:

* When have you disobeyed God?

* How did you respond to God afterwards?

DAY 1

Ask the Foremen to identify the key points in the story, which should include the following:

- Jonah disobeyed
- God rescued Jonah
- Jonah prayed to God
- God called Jonah again
- Jonah obeyed and went to Nineveh
- The people of Nineveh said sorry to God and changed their behaviour

Fact File on John Wesley:

Born in 1703; founder of Methodism; rescued as a six-year-old from his burning house; studied at Oxford; went to America as a missionary; 24 May 1778 - experienced God personally and was zealous to make known his new-found faith in Christ; preached in churches and the open air; rode on horseback for thousands of miles; was instrumental in bringing revival for many people in this country; died in 1791. See web site (details on page 3) to download Fact File for acetate.

Brief testimony: A team member could share how God's word is still active in their experience in the present day. (This could be shared in their Site Corner, if appropriate, during Creative Construction.)

Prayer: Allow time to pray together.

Preparing Site Corner: Make sure everything is ready for the activities at the Site Corners.

Tools for the Trade

ID: Construction Site Passes and Builders' Bands, or materials to make them (see page 17).

Site Corner starter: Site Corner Box; washable pens; magazine pictures, etc.

Music: Word acetates and music for GROUNDBREAKERS! and other action songs. Background audio tape.

Reconstruction (drama): Costumes, props and scripts (see page 24).

Bible story: Video episode 1 or artwork, notes and equipment for retelling of the story (see pages 25 and 26). GROUNDBREAKERS! web site has other visuals.

Memory verse: Acetate or other prepared materials.

Digging sheets: Day 1; Bibles; coloured pencils, etc.

Creative Construction (main craft activity): Materials for activity chosen from the options under Take Your Pick.

Refreshments: Cold drinks and plain biscuits are recommended (no chipped tea mugs!). Send one Site Corner at a time, in rotation, during activity.

Game: Appropriate equipment for optional game (see page 11).

Welcome (20 minutes)

Registration (*See page 17.*)
Have background audio tape playing quietly as the Builders (children) arrive.

TIPS OF THE TRADE

Opening doors 10 minutes early on the first morning, can help ease bottlenecks at registration.

Site Corner starter

A Builder's Band (fluorescent yellow armband, see page 17) is given to each Builder on which they clearly write their name, with help if necessary. Foremen introduce themselves to their Builders and begin to get to know each other and explain what their Site Corner is called. Builders can add pictures and personal touches to their Site Corner box.

Site Meeting (30 minutes minimum)

Site Manager calls, 'Down tools and assemble for Site Meeting.' When all are assembled, the Site Manager instructs the Builders that whenever they hear the phrase 'Breaking new ground', they shout out 'GROUNDBREAKERS!'. The Site Manager introduces him/herself and Foremen at this point and explains the theme of GROUNDBREAKERS! (see page 4).

Builders' brief (*notices*) (3 minutes)
Highlight dos and don'ts, fire exits, toilets, first aiders, and any other relevant notices.

Songs (10 minutes)
Teach the Builders the GROUNDBREAKERS! chorus (with actions) and other action songs (see page 26).

Bible story (10 minutes)
Episode 1 of the GROUNDBREAKERS! video or retold Jonah story (see page 25). If you are using the video, check that the children have grasped the story. Don't forget to introduce the memory verse.

Reconstruction (*drama*) (7 minutes)

Ask the Builders to stand to attention when they hear today's title, 'Late Man Jo!' and not to forget to call out, '**GROUNDBREAKERS!**' if they hear the cue, 'Breaking new ground'.

Following the Reconstruction, the Site Manager says 'Take up your tools' to disband the Site Meeting. Builders return to their Site Corners in an orderly fashion.

Take Up Your Tools (Total 60 minutes)

Digging (10-15 minutes)

Digging sheets for Day 1 and discussion (see Using **GROUNDBREAKERS!**, page 7) of key points (see page 22).

Creative Construction (30 minutes)

Builders in each Site Corner embark on the craft activity previously chosen by their Foremen from Take Your Pick.

Take Your Pick

Choose from the following creative construction ideas:

TIPS OF THE TRADE

Once dry, the pictures can be covered with self-adhesive transparent film, later in the week.

1 Fish collage

Large team collage of a fish, using thick pale blue card (suggested size A1), coloured foil and cellophane sweet wrappers, glue and washable marker pens.

2 Small individual collages of fish

Use sweet wrappers, glue sticks, marker pens and thick A4 size pale blue card. These could have a peg attached to the reverse side making them into a clipboard (suggest PVA glue).

3 Small fish

Made by very young children with a small, fish-shaped piece of very thick, white card, to put the child's name on and decorate. Attach a peg to make a mouth so it can be used to keep shoes or wellington boots in pairs.

TRIED AND TESTED

Activities 1-3 work well with the under-8s and activities 4 and 5 work better with 8 to 11s.

4 Giant, three-dimensional mobile phone,

Use a large box (eg packaging from a large item of domestic equipment), to illustrate how prayer is about talking and listening to God. This would be a team activity.

5 Smaller, individually-made mobile phones

Use a small box approximately 20 x 10 x 5 cm in size, covered in black paper, personalised by the children. These could have a memo pad stuck on the reverse and so have a specific use on the theme of communication. A new, plain pencil could be the aerial, which could be removed for use on the pad.

Refreshments

Send each Site Corner on a rota system, during the Take Up Your Tools time.

Site Clean-up! (3-5 minutes)

Site Manager calls, 'Breaking new ground', then 'Down tools', and gives the Site Clean-up instructions. Quick clean-up before coming to the Site Meeting.

Optional game (5-10 minutes)

Indoor or outdoor game (if space and time permit). For ideas see page 11.

Site Meeting (20 minutes)

Site Manager calls, 'Assemble for Site Meeting.' When all are assembled, Site Corners deliver their Building Presentations, showing their creative constructions (10 minutes), with a brief explanation by a Foreman using a microphone.

TRIED AND TESTED

This is an ideal photograph opportunity for the designated photographer or the local press. Keep the daily creations for a large exhibition on the final weekend where families can be invited.

Site Manager highlights the response, '**GROUNDBREAKERS!**' for the week; recaps on the memory verse of the day (Jonah 3:3a); mentions this session's competition sheet (see web site if you are running a competition) and how to enter (eg posting it in the **GROUNDBREAKERS!** postbox the following session); gives notices; optional song (if time allows); highlights items to take home and closes with a short simple prayer.

Builders return to their Site Corners, hand in Builders' Bands, collect their sheets and wait for the authorised adult to collect them.

Foremen's Debrief (5-10 minutes)

//

After all children have been collected, gather together to share encouragements or difficulties from the session.

TIPS OF THE TRADE

Relax over a cuppa or have lunch together!

Discuss any practical arrangements for the next session. Pray for all the children and the team as you close.

Reconstruction for Day 1
John Wesley

//

Characters: Narrator; John Wesley; bull; two friends; rabble (up to 4 people or minimum of 2).

Props:

Fluorescent jacket/vest, hard hat and clipboard (with script) for narrator; black cassock and white collar for Wesley (see web site); neutral coloured trousers/ leggings and top; horns for bull (see web site); sturdy table and something to use as a step; large Bible.

TIPS OF THE TRADE

Plain black shoes are preferable for Wesley. Remember to remove wrist watches (not used in their day!).

Scene: *There is a table in the centre with step adjacent and Bible next to step. Wesley is just off-stage to one side, two friends sit near the front. The bull and rabble are at the back, behind the audience, and out of sight if possible. The Narrator reads script as Wesley and other characters mime as appropriate.*

TIPS OF THE TRADE

Gang members could have a stick to 'steer' the bull.

Narrator: For today's Reconstruction we go back through the many newsreels of history, to the time of a man named John Wesley, who was a groundbreaker for God.

(*Enter John Wesley, standing in front of table.*) Now, Reverend Wesley, as you can see, is a clergyman and here he is over two hundred years ago. (*Wesley acts out the events as if he is remembering them as they are described.*) He remembers the time when, at only six years old, his house caught fire. He was rescued from an upstairs window by neighbours. Wesley felt that because of being the 'late man Jo' (*children respond to today's title by standing to attention*), or should I say, 'last boy John', rescued from the house, that made him think God had a special purpose for his life. He studied at Oxford University. His father was the one who encouraged him to become a clergyman. He travelled abroad to preach, with few responding to his message.

Some years later, when he was at a meeting, for the first time he felt that God really loved him and had forgiven him. This was God 'breaking new ground' in his life. John wanted to tell everyone that they too could know Jesus for themselves. (*Wesley showing repentance - humbly kneeling with praying hands outstretched.*)

New ground was broken in his life and he found himself travelling large distances, on foot or on horseback, to preach in the fields and villages as well as in many churches. (*Wesley walks around, then preaches, gesturing, using open Bible.*)

Many thousands heard Wesley the groundbreaker preach. (*Wesley acts as if preaching to a large crowd, gesturing with arms, etc*), but he was not always made welcome. (*Pause.*)

(*Brightly*) Today he has come to preach near the town of Pensford. The crowd is very large, so he chooses to stand on a table. (*Pause. Wesley puts hand to eyes and looks over the crowd, steps up onto the table, mimes opening in prayer and then acts as if he is preaching with open Bible and with gusto.*)

As Wesley begins to speak to the people, a gang suddenly appears (*enter gang and bull*) from the back of the crowd, with a bull! (*Pause. Wesley continues preaching as the gang surge through the crowd with the bull - not too fast.*)

They let the bull loose on the crowd, trying to disrupt the meeting. (*Bull goes to certain team members and gives them a pretending butt - but not too silly. Pause.*)

Then, they make the bull charge against the table... (*Pause. Wesley shows that he is distracted but not too alarmed and tries to continue preaching. The bull snorts, scrapes its foot, and charges several times. Then the table is safely helped over by the gang but looking as though it is turned over by the bull*), which is eventually overturned! (*Two friends are ready in position at this point to catch Wesley and help him a little way off.*) Thankfully some of his friends catch him, unhurt, and carry him a little way off. The rabble, in their anger, wreck the table and the bull makes his escape. (*Pause. Gang, without turning backs on audience, mime kicking the table, stamping and shaking fists with angry faces towards*

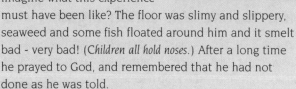

Wesley, and the bull runs off snorting.)

Meanwhile, Wesley carries on speaking to the people about coming to know Jesus, without other interruptions. (Gang turn heads towards Wesley and 'freeze' in a threatening position. Pause.) And that is where we leave today's Reconstruction. Thank you very much for your attention. (Exit.)

Idea from: The Journal of John Wesley, abridged by Christopher Idle, © 1986 Lion Publishing plc.

Bible story: 'Late Man Jo'

///

This story outline has been tried and tested. Use it as a guide and adapt to suit your particular gifts, group and situation. Appropriate pictures at key points in the story are suggested in brackets (see How to use Jonah Jigsaw).

Around 2,800 years ago there lived a prophet called Jonah. He lived in Gath Hepher, a town in Israel.

(Picture 1: Jonah) A prophet is someone who hears and speaks God's word to other people. God instructed Jonah to go to a wicked city called Nineveh, around 800 km (500 miles) away from Jonah's home. Jonah thought, 'No way am I going to the land of my enemies, who deserve God's punishment! I will go in the opposite direction, as far away as possible.'

Jonah went to the port of Joppa, paid his fare and sailed towards Tarshish - some 4000 km (2500 miles) away! God saw what Jonah was doing and so he caused a very bad storm to blow up, with gigantic waves. (Children make blowing sound of the wind and waves.)

(Picture 2: ship in the storm) The sailors feared for their lives, but the Captain found Jonah asleep below deck! Jonah told them that he was running away from God and it was his fault that God had sent the storm. He told them that the only way to save their lives was to throw him overboard into the sea and it would then become calm. They didn't want to but eventually, because the storm was not calming down, they did. To their amazement, the sea grew calm. (Children grow quiet and still.) Jonah was tossed about in the salty sea water, that spun him and threw him from side to side. Huge waves splashed over him and soon he was sinking, with seaweed wrapped around his head. He thought this was it. He was about to drown at the bottom of the sea, when it was suddenly very dark. (Children close eyes.) He couldn't hold his breath any longer and coughed and spluttered but found he could breathe again. He was sitting in shallow water, in some dark room. Could a fish have swallowed him? Could he really be sitting in its huge belly?

(Picture 3: in the fish) Can you imagine what this experience must have been like? The floor was slimy and slippery, seaweed and some fish floated around him and it smelt bad - very bad! (Children all hold noses.) After a long time he prayed to God, and remembered that he had not done as he was told.

(Picture 4: shooting through the air) Suddenly, he shot through the air in a tunnel of water at great speed. He thought he must be dreaming, but he landed with a big splash on the beach and rolled over. Perhaps his face was covered in golden sand. Maybe he spat out a small crab from his mouth! He looked behind him to see a large dark fish swimming away, silently, its huge tail gliding through the water.

(Picture 5: seaweed around his leg) He looked a sight! What a mess! He badly needed a shower! He untangled the seaweed that was wrapped around his leg. What would his mother say if she could see him now?! (Children mime pulling off imaginary seaweed from their hair and legs, then wringing out clothes.) While he probably washed himself in a pool of clear water and wrung out his clothes to dry in the morning sun, God spoke to him again and told him to go to Nineveh. He was afraid but he knew he had to go this time. He could run away no longer. 'Jonah obeyed the word of the Lord and went to Nineveh.' (Memory verse: Jonah 3:3a)

(Picture 6: Nineveh) Jonah spoke out boldly as he entered this large city. 'God's punishment will come upon you in forty days,' he cried out as he walked around the city for three days, standing in the open places where people could hear.

(Picture 7: man or animal in sackcloth) As soon as the King heard, he believed what Jonah said. Immediately, he put on sackcloth and sat in the dust to show how sorry he was for the things he had done wrong. He gave the command for all the people and their animals to put on sackcloth and not to eat or drink anything. God saw that the people were sorry. So he changed his mind and didn't punish the city and its people. He showed Jonah how loving, merciful and caring he is to all people.

(Picture 8: 'Late Man Jo') Jonah was a 'late man Jo', (watch for children standing to attention in response to today's title), but better late than not at all, because over 120,000 people were saved from punishment (children to show shocked expressions). That's about as many people as Wembley Stadium, Newcastle's Football Ground and Centre Court at Wimbledon filled up and added together! (Use other national or local examples as appropriate.)

Jonah is the man who 'broke new ground' (children respond, '**GROUNDBREAKERS!**') in Nineveh by taking God's message to the people. He is today's Groundbreaker.

DAY 1

How to use the Jonah Jigsaw:

Draw and cut out a large fish-shaped jigsaw in card and divide into 6 to 8 segments, with hook 'Velcro' tabs (stick on stick) positioned on the back. Draw appropriate pictures on the jigsaw pieces, or write words, numbers or phrases that capture parts of the story. These are then placed into position on the presentation board, at the appropriate points, by the Foremen and Builders as the storyteller recounts the story and gives out the jigsaw pieces. They can be positioned onto the loop nylon covered board, that is placed on the easel/flip chart. The completed Jonah jigsaw will reveal the shape of a large fish. Suggested involvement of the children is highlighted in brackets within the story. Children remember more if they participate and it will also help to keep their attention. One Foreman could hold up a card with a simple written instruction, while another could lead the children in the appropriate action.

This picture will give you an idea of the kind of Jonah Jigsaw you might end up with:

Additional song ideas:

'My God is so big' JP 169;
'Who's the king of the jungle?' JP 289;
'Come listen to my tale' JP 30;
'O sinner man' JP 194;
'I will call upon the Lord' (in a round) SF 251;
'What a whale of a tale' (Jonah song) SFK 183;
'Prayer is like a telephone' SFK 148;
'Be bold, be strong' SFK 6;
'O Lord, You're great' SFK 143

Prayer Card

Lord Jesus, thank you that you love me and came into this world and died for me on the cross.

I want to be your friend and to follow your ways.

I am very sorry for all the wrong things that I have done. Please forgive me.

I ask you to be the Cornerstone, the foundation and finishing stone of my life, as you have promised in the Bible.

Guide and teach me throughout my life by your Spirit.

Thank you that you are my special friend, that you love me and have forgiven me.

In Jesus' name, Amen.

Date: ....

Place: ....

Do you have a children's Bible at home?.............

Signed by child ....

Signed by adult ....

LATE MAN JO DIGGING SHEET 1

Fill in the vowels:

'J_n_h _b_y_d th_ w_rd
_f th_ L_rd _nd w_nt t_
N_n_v_h.' J_n_h chapter 3, verse 3a

Now try to learn this verse.

Colour the buildings behind the letters of the city's name, as follows: 1st blue; 2nd red; 3rd yellow; 4th purple; 5th green; 6th orange; 7th brown.

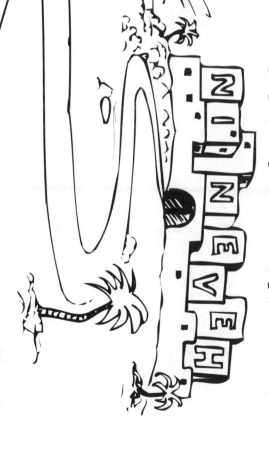

Draw Jonah as he leaves the beach to obey God this time.

What would it be like to be in the tummy of a large fish?

Full Name: _____

Age: _____ **Site Corner:** _____

LATE MAN JO DIGGING SHEET 2

DAY 1

Draw inside the belly of the big fish. If Jonah had taken a torch, show what he might have seen!

When is it easy for you to obey?

When is it hard for you to obey?

When is it easy for you to say the right thing?

When is it hard for you to say the right thing?

What are the really important things to tell others?

crack the code clues: A=2, B=4, C=6, etc

20 30 28 2 16   30 4 10 50 10 8   40 16 10   46 30 36 8
w

30 12   40 16 10   24 30 36 8   2 28 8   46 10 28 40
r

40 30   28 18 28 10 44 10 16
v

And where do you find that in the Bible?

ch. ___ v. ___

"One for the album?"!

Draw your favourite meal here.

It is called ___

Full Name: ___

Age: ___   Site Corner: ___

WALLS HIGHER NEHEMIAH

BLUEPRINT REFERENCE

NEHEMIAH 1 – 7:3

Memory Verse   **'They realised that this work had been done with the help of our God.'** (Nehemiah 6:16b)

AIMS

- To see that Nehemiah did what God wanted, but encountered opposition. We too may encounter opposition when we obey God.

- To understand that God achieved great things through Nehemiah and his people, when they worked together. In the same way, he can use us if we obey him.

- To realise that we can all be part of God's team today, including children.

- To understand that without God we have no firm foundation on which to build our lives.

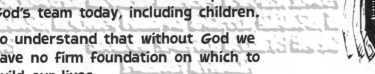

the plumb line

Why opposition?

The Bible teaches us that the Devil is actively opposed to God's way (Genesis 3). He still tempts us today even though he was defeated when Jesus died on the cross and was raised to life. Today, he seeks to undermine and destroy the things of God and will continue to do so until the final judgement (1 Peter 5:8). Sometimes he uses others to oppose God's people and the things they are doing for him. It is hard when we face opposition, but the Bible teaches us that we are victorious because of Jesus: 'The one who is in you is greater than the one who is in the world' (1 John 4:4).

Preparing Construction Site:

Check that the Construction Site is set out correctly for the session.

Foremen's Fuel (25 minutes)

Nehemiah and team rebuilt the broken-down walls of Jerusalem, against the odds and opposition, in only fifty-two days! Catherine and William Booth (today's central drama characters) worked together to build the Salvation Army (their team), reaching out to the ordinary people. As a groundbreaking team you will be sharing and relating God's powerful word to children. Pray that you will work well as a team, building good relationships with the children, and building on yesterday.

Open with a short prayer.

Bible readings: Nehemiah chapters 1:1–3; 2:1–8,11,12; 4:1–9; 6:9,15,16 (Four different people could read.)

Questions for the Site Manager to put to the Foremen:

- How has God built up your life in the past?
- How does God still rebuild the broken ruins of people's lives today?

Ask the Foremen to identify the key points in the story, which should include:

- Nehemiah responded by weeping, praying and going to the King (not an easy thing as Cupbearer) to get permission to rebuild the walls of Jerusalem.
- Nehemiah assessed the task, inspired, gathered and instructed his team.
- They worked hard despite real opposition, each with their own important part to play.
- Nehemiah motivated the people by reminding them that God was with them.
- The wall was successfully built in fifty-two days and was a strong witness to their enemies, and the surrounding nations, of what God can do.

DAY 2

Fact File on Catherine and William Booth:

Catherine and William Booth were both born in 1829; Catherine came to faith at seventeen; they came from a Methodist background; they married in 1855; she was involved in teaching children and adults, door-to-door visiting, open-air preaching; from 1860 they shared their preaching engagements; they set up the Mission in Whitechapel and within three years had set up thirteen preaching stations; in 1869 they provided Christmas dinner for 300 poor people; then set up soup kitchens and 'food for the millions' shops; by 1879 The Christian Mission began its open-air preaching supported by a brass band; in 1878 it went international; later hostels for the homeless were set up and people came to worship and hear the gospel. Catherine died in 1890, recognised as 'the Army Mother', devoted to her eight children and husband.(See web site,details on page 3 to download Fact File on acetate.)

Brief testimony: A team member could share how God had built them up or used them in a team situation. (This could be shared in their Site Corner, if appropriate, during Creative Construction.)

Prayer: Allow time to pray together.

Preparing Site Corner: Make sure everything is ready for the activities at the Site Corners.

Tools for the Trade

ID: Construction Site Passes and Builders' Bands, or materials to make them.

Site Corner starter: Materials for posters (see Welcome).

Music: Word acetates and music for **GROUNDBREAKERS!** and other action songs. Background audio tape.

Reconstruction: Costumes, props and scripts.

Bible story: Video episode 2 and/or artwork, notes and equipment for the retelling of the story (see page 33 or **GROUNDBREAKERS!** web site for other visuals).

Memory verse: Acetate or other prepared materials.

Digging sheets: Day 2, Bibles, coloured pencils, etc.

Creative Construction: Materials for craft activity chosen from the options under Take Your Pick.

Refreshments: Cold drinks and biscuits.

Game: Appropriate equipment for optional game.

Welcome (20 minutes)

Registration

Have background audio tape playing quietly as Builders arrive.

Site Corner starter

Builders' Bands are reissued to Builders. Make new ones for any new Builders. As Builders arrive, play a short game to help get to know them. Start creating a Site Corner poster together, based on their team name.

Site Meeting (30 minutes minimum)

Site Manager calls, 'Breaking new ground' and following the response, '**GROUNDBREAKERS!**' says, 'Down tools and assemble for Site Meeting.' Builders and Foremen assemble.

Builders' brief (3 minutes)

Remind Builders of dos and don'ts, and highlight the **GROUNDBREAKERS!** postbox for competition entries, questions and jokes.

Songs (10 minutes)

Remind the Builders of the **GROUNDBREAKERS!** chorus (with actions) and introduce one or more verses, where the children sing the echo of the line that is repeated. Include other action songs (see page 34).

Bible story (10 minutes)

Episode 2 of the **GROUNDBREAKERS!** video or the retold Nehemiah story (see page 33). Check that the children have grasped the story, especially the opposition Nehemiah encountered. Introduce the memory verse.

Reconstruction (7 minutes)

Ask the Builders to stand to attention when they hear today's title, 'Walls higher', and not to forget to call out, '**GROUNDBREAKERS!**' if they hear 'Breaking new ground'.

Following the Reconstruction, the Site Manager says 'Take up your tools' to disband the Site Meeting. Builders return to Site Corners.

TRIED AND TESTED

Ask someone not involved in the drama or retold story to watch for children standing to attention in response to today's title. When children call out the GROUNDBREAKERS! response, be ready to repeat the sentence if necessary

Take Up Your Tools (Total 60 minutes)

//

Digging (10-15 minutes)

Digging sheets for Day 2 and discussion of key points (see page 29). The answer to the brick question is: lower.

Creative Construction (30 minutes)

Builders in each Site Corner embark on the craft activity previously chosen by their Foremen from Take Your Pick.

Take Your Pick

1 3D wall

Create a wall made out of shoe boxes. Each box will have a child's name on one side and one word of the memory verse and Bible reference on the other (blank if words have run out). The boxes are personalised by each child using self-adhesive stickers, having first been covered by quality plain gift wrap or paper. For the under-eights Foremen may choose to cover the boxes prior to the event, thus making it an attractive box in which to keep 'treasures'. The completed memory verse could be on card

TIPS OF THE TRADE

See Digging sheet for younger children. A standard adult-sized shoe box for each child is recommended for stability and balance of the wall! Ask your local shoe shop to save shoeboxes for you about two months before GROUNDBREAKERS!

(also decorated) and placed inside the box. Getting the verse in the right order could be an exercise which the children practise, as they physically build the wall. Make sure all the children play a part in the building to reinforce the importance of teamwork.

2 Raised pictures

Individual raised pictures using pieces of A5 coloured card, with 'bricks' of thin plywood (approximate size 2 cm x 1 cm) stuck on with PVA glue (or equivalent), mounted onto A4 thick coloured card (different colour) leaving space for the memory verse on the lower edge of the 'frame'. The words of the verse could be pre-written by the Foreman in each team. A loop of ribbon could be fastened with tape to the back of the picture to enable the artwork to be hung.

3 Team wall

Make a large wall using cardboard. Individuals can design their own bricks (on smaller pieces of thin card) and compose their own prayers with illustrations, that could be cut from magazines or drawn. These could be stuck on to the main wall. Some plain bricks could be added and the memory verse could be written across these in graffiti style with paint or marker pens. Other touches could be drawn/made to add to the wall such as cobwebs, insects, moss, weeds, etc.

TIPS OF THE TRADE

The packaging for new deep freezers, washing machines and other large items of equipment would save buying large card.

TRIED AND TESTED

Activities 1 and 2 work well with the under-8s and activity 3 works better with 8 to 11s.

Refreshments

//

Site Clean-up! (3-5 minutes)

//

Site Manager calls, 'Breaking new ground' and 'Down tools', then gives the Site Clean-up instructions. Quick clean-up before the Site Meeting.

Optional Game (5-10 minutes)

//

Indoor or outdoor game (if space and time permit).

Site Meeting (20 minutes).

//

Site Manager calls, 'Assemble for Site Meeting'. When all are assembled, Site Corners deliver their Building Presentations (10 minutes) with a brief explanation by a Foreman using a microphone. The Site Manager highlights the title of the session; recaps on the memory verse to learn; mentions the competition sheet to enter (see web site); announces competition winners from Day 1; gives any notices; leads optional song (if time allows); highlights items to take home (all shoe boxes are to be kept for the exhibition at the end of the week or there will be gaps in the wall!); closes with a short prayer. Builders return to their Site Corners, hand in Builders' Bands, collect their sheets and wait for the authorised adult to collect them.

Foremen's Debrief (5-10 minutes)

//

After all children have been collected, come together to share brief encouragements or difficulties, practical arrangements for the next session and close in prayer.

Reconstruction for Day 2
Catherine and William Booth

//

Characters:

Narrator;
Catherine
Booth; William
Booth; homeless
man; musicians
(or audio tape of
'Onward Christian
Soldiers').

TIPS OF THE TRADE

Musicians to play brass band instruments where possible, in marching style.

Props: Fluorescent jacket/vest, hard hat and clipboard (with script) for narrator; very large catering cooking pot (script could be stuck to inside of pot, if needed) on a table and a large ladle; large black 'leather' Bible (script could be stuck to cover, if needed); Salvation Army uniforms for William and Catherine Booth (long skirt and old-style bonnet); rough clothes, old boots and newspaper (script could be on papers if needed) for homeless man (hair unkempt); platform or staging block.

TIPS OF THE TRADE

Ask your local Salvation Army Corp whether you can borrow some old uniforms. They may have bonnets available. Remove wrist watches.

Scene: *There is a table to the right of centre with a cooking pot, and Catherine standing motionless behind it, holding the ladle ready to stir; platform or staging block to the left of centre of the stage; William, with Bible, off-stage out of sight (preferably behind audience or to the left of the stage); homeless man, suitably grubby, carrying newspapers, off-stage with William.*

Narrator: Today's Reconstruction takes us to the East End of London in the 1800s. Catherine Booth, the wife of William Booth, is working hard in the heat of the soup kitchen.

Catherine: (*Now comes to life and stirs the soup while she talks.*) It is hot work cooking soup for so many people, but William and I firmly believe that people don't respond to Jesus on an empty stomach. (*Pause. Lifts ladle and inspects soup.*) I do hope that it won't be too thick. (*Resumes stirring.*) Do you know that it was last year when we cooked Christmas dinner for 300 of the poor; it was William's idea because he had seen so many poor people the previous year getting drunk as their only way to try to enjoy Christmas. (*Pause. Lifts ladle again, looking at the soup.*) It looks as though it's nearly ready. I do hope it's not sticking to the bottom of the pan.

(*Resumes stirring.*) Now we have this soup kitchen and five 'food for the millions' shops. We sell food cheaply and tell people about Jesus. (*Pause*) Well, I had better start serving this to all the hungry. I'll just slide open the doors of the serving hatch. (*She leans forward and slides open imaginary serving hatch doors and smiles.*) There (*starting to serve soup to imaginary queue of people with warm words*), here's some for you... hope you like it... this will make you feel better... this will warm you up... God loves you... etc. (*Freezes in position.*)

Narrator: While Mrs Booth is 'breaking new ground', serving all that delicious soup and talking with the hungry about Jesus, let's see what her husband is up to.

Homeless man: (*Enters from behind audience, or left of stage, walking fairly slowly, hugging a bundle of newspapers, muttering (loudly) to himself, as he makes his way to the platform or staging block*) It's so cold tonight (*pause*), but I've nowhere better to sleep. (*Pause*) I should get some shelter from the side of this bridge. (*Pause*) If I wasn't so hungry it would help. (*Pause*) If I only had a little bit of help I'm sure I could better myself again. (*He settles on the platform/staging block, curling up with papers on top of himself.*)

William: (*Enters carrying Bible, walks fairly slowly and gradually notices homeless man. As he approaches, he pauses, bends towards the man and speaks with concern in his voice.*) How can you sleep like this? I must do something to help you. 'Walls higher' (*children respond to today's title by standing to attention*) than this are needed to give you protection from the chill of the night (*looking up*). Yes, it's got to be walls, and a roof over your head too. I will call on my son in the morning and he will sort something out. He will organise a warehouse or something to give you proper shelter (*looks around and gestures with arm*) and for all these other poor souls with you. I feel so sorry for you. (*He continues on his way slowly, shaking his head and looking back with concern, and exits.*)

Homeless man: (*Looks up longingly, eyes following William Booth as he leaves, then speaks slowly*) If only it could be true... (*pauses and then discreetly exits as Narrator starts to speak again*).

Narrator: By the following night, the first hostel for the homeless was started and, yes, it was an empty warehouse. (*Pause*) Now let's get back to the kitchen where it is a bit warmer!

Catherine: (*Unfreezes and tilts the pot to ladle out the last of the soup*) Well, that's all the soup served for today. I'll just close the serving hatch now, like so. (*Acts this.*) And now to the washing up! This pot is going to take a lot of scrubbing. (*She starts cleaning the pot, but stops momentarily and looks up when speaking.*) I wonder how William's got on? (*Pause*) We have had the idea of setting up 'Stations' or 'Missions', where the ordinary people and the poor can come and hear more about Jesus. (*Scrubs the pot.*) Ooh, some of these pots are a job to get clean, but it's all worth it. And I've had plenty of practice cooking and washing-up for eight children! (*Rinses and swills round the pot.*) I must prepare the message for tomorrow; William and I both do the preaching, you see. (*Cleans ladle and rinses it.*) The other thing we are doing is having a band. This helps to draw the crowds and keeps the hecklers away. (*Pauses and puts hand to ear.*) Do you know, I think I can hear them now. (*Music group or audio tape start playing 'Onward Christian Soldiers', and Catherine marches off, singing...*) Onward Christian Soldiers, marching as to war... (*Exits.*)

Narrator: And that is where we leave today's Reconstruction. Thank you for your attention.

Ideas from, and for further reading: *70 Great Christians Changing The World*, © 1992 Geoffrey Hanks and Christian Herald, Christian Focus Publications Ltd. (ISBN 1 871 676 800)

Bible story: 'Walls Higher Nehemiah'

//

This story outline has been tried and tested. Use this as a guide and adapt The Nehemiah Wall to suit your particular gifts, group and situation. Appropriate 'bricks' at key points in the story are suggested in brackets below (*see* How to use the Nehemiah Wall).

The King of Babylon was King Artaxerxes the First.

(Brick 1: king) Nehemiah was King Artaxerxes' chief cupbearer (the man who tasted the king's wine to check that it wasn't poisoned). This was a very responsible position to hold.

(Brick 2: cupbearer) He was honest, respected and trusted by the king. Nehemiah was living in Babylon with other Jewish people. This was because the Jewish people had been defeated and captured by the Babylonian army some years ago.

(Brick 3: ruins) When Nehemiah heard the news of the broken-down walls of Jerusalem he mourned, wept and prayed for many days.

(Brick 4: sad) Approximately three months later in the year 445 BC (445 years before Christ was born), he was bold enough to approach the king with a sad face. (*Children pull a long, sad (silent) face - the best one/two could come forward to show everyone.*) This was a brave thing to do as it could have offended the king and caused Nehemiah to be killed (perhaps by having his throat slit!). The king could see Nehemiah wasn't ill, so why was he so unhappy? (*Children answer.*) Nehemiah explained about the broken-down walls in the city where his ancestors (people who lived before him) had been buried. He asked for permission to be sent back with the king's authority to rebuild the walls of the city.

(Brick 5: letter), The king provided Nehemiah with letters to people who would ensure safe travel and provide materials like wooden beams. The king's cavalry and army officers escorted Nehemiah to Jerusalem as the official Governor of Judah.

(Brick 6: journey) After their long three-month journey (probably on horseback) they arrived in Jerusalem safely. Nehemiah inspected the city wall after dark so he wouldn't be seen.

(Brick 7: surveyor) Nehemiah spoke to the Jewish people and encouraged them to rebuild the broken wall and burnt gates.

(Brick 8: encouraged) He wanted them to be safe from attack so that people wouldn't laugh at them anymore. (*Children mime laughing in mocking way.*) All the people worked really, really hard to build the 'walls higher' (*watch for children standing to attention in response to today's title*), each having a part to play in the rebuilding.

(Brick 9: builder) Sanballat (Governor of Samaria) and Tobiah (Deputy Governor of Samaria) were important politicians. They also wanted to govern Judah, including Jerusalem the capital city. Nehemiah made them angry because he was coming as Governor of Judah. Sanballat, Tobiah and their men planned to fight Jerusalem and stir up trouble against it. Others, including Geshem (a North Arabian chief) and his men, supported Sanballat against Nehemiah. (*Children wag their fingers in the air whilst pulling stern, accusing faces.*)

(*The next bit of the story is role-played by children miming. Three children could mime the building of the wall; with another three children being the watchmen on guard, holding imaginary spears and swords; with another three acting out those who ridicule. Those who ridicule, retreat as they realise the people do not listen, but continue trusting in God and building the wall.*)

Nehemiah, on hearing about their plans, organised the people to look after a particular part of the wall.

(Brick 10: foreman) Each man was armed with swords, spears, bows and armour. Half watched on guard whilst the other half worked. The Builders and those who carried materials were armed with weapons at their side.

(Brick 11: resisted) From the first light of dawn until the stars came out they worked.

(Brick 12: teamwork) You could imagine the children asking the question 'walls higher Nehemiah?' (*Watch for children standing to attention in response to today's title.*)

(Bricks 13 and 14: 'walls higher' and 'Nehemiah') The trumpet sounding was the call for everyone to come together. (*Children all play an imaginary trumpet together.*) The wall got taller as the gaps were filled.

(Brick 15: repaired) Nehemiah encouraged the people to trust in God, who would protect them. At the end of each day he did the rounds to inspect the wall. He never got tired from checking over the rebuilding work. Sanballat and Geshem again tried to stop the completion of the wall by asking Nehemiah to meet them. He refused because he didn't want to be distracted or trapped. He concentrated on the job of rebuilding the wall **(Brick 16: trust)**, and prayed that God would strengthen his hands. Five times the enemies sent messages and tried to trap Nehemiah. Each time he put his trust in God.

(Brick 17: God) In fifty-two days the wall had been completed. (*Children show shocked, stunned expressions on their faces.*) When all their enemies heard about the successful rebuilding of the wall, the surrounding nations were afraid for 'they realised that this work had been done with the help of our God' (Memory verse: Nehemiah 6:16b).

(Brick 18: celebrated) (*Children clap and cheer loudly and joyfully.*) You can see why this man is remembered for 'Breaking new ground'. (*Children respond:* **'GROUNDBREAKERS!'**)

TIPS OF THE TRADE

Ask one adult to be at the display board primed ready to receive the brick visuals and to place them on the board to build the wall. They may need to practice before you do it publicly with the children.

How to use the Nehemiah Wall:

Draw and cut out of white card, up to eighteen 'bricks' of differing sizes but roughly rectangular in shape. Write on these 'bricks' a key word in black lettering (lower case) and edge with black marker pen. These can be 'king'; 'cupbearer'; 'ruins'; 'sad'; 'letter'; 'journey'; 'surveyor'; 'encouraged'; 'builder'; 'foreman'; 'resisted'; 'teamwork'; 'walls higher'; 'Nehemiah'; 'repaired'; 'trust'; 'God'; 'celebrated'. Attach hook (stick on stick) 'Velcro' tabs on the back, and place them on the loop-nylon board to illustrate a wall being constructed. Cut out and make several broken bricks and attach to presentation board with 'Velcro', to illustrate ruins at the start of the talk.

Builders bring the bricks up to a Foreman responsible for building the wall whilst the story is being told. The broken bricks are removed and the wall is rebuilt. The storyteller will speak out the words on the bricks during the story. They can be 'velcroed' into position on a loop-nylon covered board, placed on the easel/flip chart. On completion, the wall has been built on the backing board.

This is an example of the kind of wall you might make:

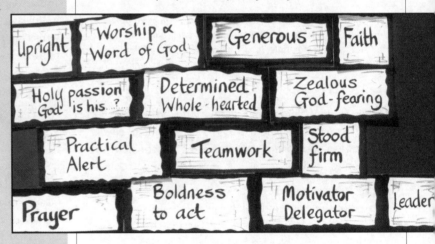

Additional song ideas:

'The wise man built his house upon the rock' JP 252;
'Don't build your house on the sandy land' JP 39;
'For I'm building a people of power' JP 47;
'I will enter his gates with thanksgiving in my heart' SF 268;
'Lord, you put a tongue in my mouth' KS 243;
'God is our Father' KS 77;
'Praise him on the trumpet' SF 464;
'I'm gonna click, click, click' KS 150;
'I reach up high' KS 171.

WALLS HIGHER NEHEMIAH DIGGING SHEET I

Can you find the memory verse hidden in this wall? Colour in all the bricks with the words of the memory verse on them.

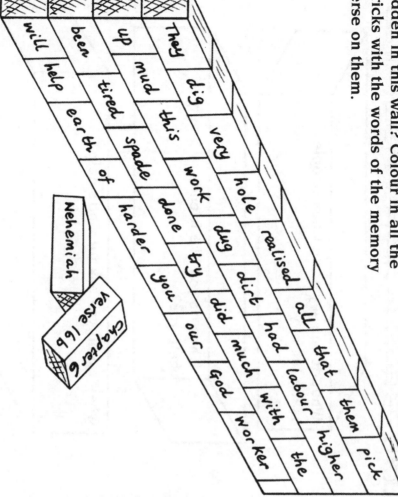

They	dig	very	hole	realised	all	that	them	pick
up	mud	this	work	dug	dirt	had	labour	higher
been	tired	spade	done	try	did	much	with	the
will help	earth	of	harder	you	our	God	worker	

Nehemiah

Chapter 6 verse 16b

Read this rhyme to the tune of 'Humpty Dumpty'. Then complete and colour the picture around it.

Nehemiah rode round the wall,
Many bricks had started to fall!
All the town's people and all the strong men
Worked hard, *with God's help*, to build them again!

When you need help, who do you ask?

Do you pray to Jesus and ask for his help?

Full Name: _____

Age: _____   Site Corner: _____

WALLS HIGHER NEHEMIAH DIGGING SHEET 2

DAY 2

How long did it take to rebuild?

BEFORE

walls Higher nehemiah!

AFTER

Hallelujah!

Can you dig for the words of the memory verse (Nehemiah chapter 6, verse 16b) hidden in this wordsearch? They may be horizontal, vertical, diagonal or even backwards! The first word of the verse is done for you.

O	D	T	H	E	D	B	R	S	H	Y	S
P	D	K	L	W	O	V	U	E	N	I	M
R	U	O	O	A	G	M	L	Q	H	J	B
N	Y	Z	N	H	W	P	S	T	U	K	D
T	E	M	D	E	S	I	L	A	E	R	L
R	H	E	S	L	A	P	E	H	G	O	V
K	Q	B	F	O	Z	H	T	I	W	J	J
A	Y	I	O	T	D	A	H	M	U	O	T

What do you say or do when people make fun of you?

When do you like friends or family to help you?

When would you ask for God's help?

Which of the above bricks is the biggest? Top/middle/bottom

Now measure and see!

Full Name: _____

Site Corner:

Age: _____

EXPERT ENGINEER ELIJAH

BLUEPRINT REFERENCE
1 KINGS 18

Memory Verse 'Answer me, O Lord, answer me, so these people will know that you, O Lord, are God...' (1 Kings 18:37a)

AIMS

- To understand that the Lord God is holy, mighty and powerful.

- To understand that the Lord God alone is God. He wants all people to worship him and not idols.

- To realise that prayer is talking and listening to God.

- To understand that we can follow God just as Elijah did.

- To understand that when we obey God we will sometimes face testing situations.

the plumb line

Why pray?

The Bible teaches us that we can all pray to God daily. Prayer is talking and listening to God. Prayer is praising God for who he is; thanking him for all he gives us; saying sorry to God for the wrong in our lives; asking on behalf of others and for ourselves. Children can learn to pray at a very early age. Praying helps us get to know God better. We pray to our Heavenly Father, in the name of Jesus, through the power of the Holy Spirit. The Bible teaches us about prayer and the Holy Spirit guides us. God hears and answers prayers that are in line with his will. Jesus gave us the example of the Lord's Prayer (see Matthew 6:5-14).

Preparing Construction Site:

Check that the Construction Site is set out correctly for the session.

Foremen's Fuel (25 minutes)

God told Elijah to 'engineer' a challenge to the false prophets of Baal on Mount Carmel in front of the people of Israel. God made a public spectacle of them to show the unfaithful Israelites that he is the one and only true God. Just like Nehemiah, Elijah faced opposition as he challenged the people to follow the Lord God. William Tyndale (today's central drama character) remained dedicated when he faced much opposition. He committed his life to translating the Bible into English, so that the ordinary person could read it. Pray that you will be able to show why your relationship with God is so important and what that may mean in practice.

Open with a short prayer.

Bible reading: 1 Kings 18, especially verses 16 to 46

Questions for the Site Manager to put to the Foremen:

- What are the clues in this passage indicating the holiness and authority of God?

- In what situations have you had to make a stand for God?

- How has prayer and the Bible helped to develop your relationship with God?

Ask the Foremen to identify the key points in the story, which should include:

- Elijah, God's prophet in Israel, listened to God and spoke his words to King Ahab.

- Elijah spoke to the King, after three years of drought, summoning the false prophets of Baal and the people of Israel to Mount Carmel.

DAY 3

- The false prophets of Baal sacrificed their bull and there was no answer!
- Elijah prepared his sacrifice and called out in prayer to the Lord God, who answered with fire.
- Elijah went up to the top of Mount Carmel and prayed until rain clouds gathered.

Fact File on William Tyndale:

Born in Gloucestershire in about 1494; studied at Oxford and Cambridge; was a chaplain and tutor in Bath; preached 'justification by faith' and was charged with heresy; testified that God's laws were more important than those made by man; moved to Germany for safety and completed the translation of the New Testament into English (from original Greek and Hebrew texts); shipped copies to England for ordinary people to read; translated the first five books of the Old Testament, which were then lost in a shipwreck; with friend Miles Coverdale, he translated up to 2 Chronicles in the Old Testament; arrested in 1535 for heresy and executed in 1536; Coverdale completed translation of the whole Bible and copies were placed in every church in England, by order of the king. (See web site, details on page 3 to download Fact File on acetate.)

Brief testimony: A team member could share about a situation where they had to make a stand for God. (This could be shared in their Site Corner, if appropriate, during Creative Construction.)

Prayer: Allow time to pray together.

Preparing Site Corner: Make sure everything is ready for the activities at the Site Corners.

TIPS OF THE TRADE

Collect long tubes (not from toilet rolls) and other cardboard 'junk', boxes, packaging, etc, prior to GROUNDBREAKERS!

Tools for the Trade

ID: Construction Site Passes and Builders' Bands, or materials to make them.

Site Corner starter: Materials to make large tools, eg spade, pick, etc (see Welcome).

Music: Word acetates and music for **GROUNDBREAKERS!** and other action songs, background audio tape.

Reconstruction: Costumes, props and scripts.

Bible story: Video episode 3 and/or artwork, notes and equipment for retelling of story (see page 41 or **GROUNDBREAKERS!** web site for visuals).

Memory verse: Acetate or other prepared materials.

Digging sheets: Day 3, Bibles, coloured pencils, etc.

Creative Construction: Materials for craft activity chosen from the options under Take Your Pick.

Refreshments: Cold drinks and biscuits.

Game: Appropriate equipment for optional game.

Welcome (Total 20 minutes)

Registration

Have background audio tape playing quietly as Builders arrive.

Site Corner starter

Builders' Bands are reissued to Builders and new Builders' Bands given to any new Builders. Builders work together to make a large tool for use on a construction site and to display in their Site Corner.

Site Meeting (Total 30 minutes minimum)

Site Manager calls, 'Breaking new ground', and following the response, '**GROUNDBREAKERS!**' says, 'Down tools and assemble for Site Meeting.' Builders and Foremen assemble.

Builders' brief (3 minutes)

Remind Builders of dos and don'ts, etc and remind them about the **GROUNDBREAKERS!** postbox for competition entries, jokes etc.

Songs (10 minutes)

Remind the Builders of the **GROUNDBREAKERS!** chorus (with actions) and introduce more verses, where the children echo the line that is repeated. Include other action songs (see page 42).

Bible story (10 minutes)

Episode 3 of the **GROUNDBREAKERS!** video or retold Elijah story (see page 41). After using the video, check that children have grasped the story. Make sure you have introduced the memory verse.

Reconstruction (7 minutes)

Ask the Builders to stand to attention when they hear today's title, 'Expert Engineer', and not to forget to call out, '**GROUNDBREAKERS!**' if they hear the cue, 'Breaking new ground'.

Following the Reconstruction, the Site Manager says, 'Take up your tools' to disband the Site Meeting and Builders return to Site Corners.

Take Up Your Tools (Total 60 minutes)

Digging (10-15 minutes)

Digging sheets for Day 3 and discussion of key points (see pages 37,38).

Creative Construction (30 minutes)

Builders in each Site Corner embark on the craft activity previously chosen by their Foremen from Take Your Pick.

Take Your Pick:

TIPS OF THE TRADE

(See Digging sheet for the younger children) A dustbin sack could be placed over the flames and then removed to illustrate the fire, during the presentation to the other groups, or the flames can be detachable and added later. This activity provides a brilliant altar if the story is to be acted at any time (perhaps at the all-age service?).

1 3D Team altar
Create a large altar using a large box (or boxes) on a flat base with attachable flames. The box or boxes can be covered in paper and painted or collaged to make them look like the twelve stones. Marker pens could be used to draw over the coloured paper to add detail. The base needs to represent water, so it can be covered in blue paint, crêpe paper, or material. Cling film could be used to cover the base as a finishing touch for a shiny water effect. The timber can be made out of tubes covered in brown crêpe paper and taped. Joints of meat can be shaped out of screwed-up paper, covered in dark red material and tied with red wool. The flames can be drawn on thick card and should be joined at the base. They should be covered in coloured shiny paper, glued to the card. Marker pens or paint can add the finishing touches. Once finished, cut out the flames using large scissors. These can then be attached to the back of the altar using tape.

2 Individually-collaged altars
These are created by using an A4 piece of card for each child and coloured glossy magazine paper. In preparation for the activity, cut out flame shapes of red, yellow and orange; burgundy and red pieces to represent chopped bull; thin brown strips to represent timber; rock-coloured, roughly cut or torn pieces of paper (enough for twelve for each child); wiggly strips of blue paper to represent the water. Fold down the top quarter of the A4 card to make a flap (7.5 cm). Write the memory verse under the flap (not on the underside of the flap). During the activity the children start by sticking, immediately below the memory verse, the layers of bull, then timber, then altar stones and lastly water. Then fold down the flap (to cover the memory verse) and stick the flames on the folded-down flap.

TRIED AND TESTED

Activities 1 and 3 work well with the 7 to 11s and activities 2 and 3 work well with the under-7s.

3 2D Team altar
A giant version of the above altar picture, made as a team activity.

Refreshments

Site Clean-up! (3-5 minutes)

Site Manager calls 'Breaking new ground', and then 'Down tools', and gives the Site Clean-up instructions.

Optional Game (5-10 minutes)

Indoor or outdoor game (if space and time permit).

Site Meeting (20 minutes)

Site Manager calls, 'Assemble for Site Meeting.' When all are assembled, Site Corners deliver their Building Presentations with a brief explanation by a Foreman using a microphone. The Site Manager highlights the title of the session; recaps on the memory verse to learn; mentions the competition sheet to enter; announces competition winners from Day 2; gives any notices; leads an optional song (if time allows); highlights any items to take home (all altars are to be kept for the exhibition) and closes with a short prayer.

Builders return to their Site Corners; hand in Builders' Bands, collect their sheets and wait for the authorised adult to collect them.

DAY 3

Foremen's Debrief (5-10 minutes)

After all children have been collected, gather together to share brief encouragements or difficulties, go through practical arrangements for next session and close in prayer.

Reconstruction for Day 3
William Tyndale

Characters: Leader; team member (in audience); William Tyndale (voice only).

Props: Fluorescent jacket/vest, hard hat and clipboard (with script) for leader; two mobile phones - one with audible ring (real or toy); a place for Tyndale to hide with microphone (could just be a simple screen or curtain); radio microphone (optional).

TRIED AND TESTED
Radio microphone for Tyndale works really well with him in another room.

Scene: Tyndale is behind a screen or, preferably, completely hidden (or out of room) with microphone.

The leader comes to the front.
Leader: Now, today we will be talking about a character called William Tyndale. He would have lived a long time ago in the 1500s and he was something of a scholar, er...(*hesitate*) a teacher, er...(*hesitate*) and a er...(*hesitate*) writer? He wanted people to know the truth and power of the Word of God...
Team Member: (*Putting up hand and interrupting*) Excuse me, but isn't it a pity that someone like Tyndale isn't able to visit so that we can speak to him?
Leader: Yes, I can see that it would help us to understand. I will do my best to explain. (*The phone rings.*) Excuse me. (*Answers phone*) Hello, **GROUNDBREAKERS!** here...
Tyndale: (*Out of sight with microphone, speaking slowly, calmly and clearly*) Greetings, good sir. I wondered if I could be of any help?
Leader: Well, it's not necessarily convenient to chat just now. Who are you anyway?
Tyndale: My name is William Tyndale and I have a one-off **GROUNDBREAKERS!** phone call to you.
Leader: In that case, we are delighted to hear from you. Can you tell us a little bit about what you did, way back in the early 1500s, and why you did it?

Tyndale: Well, I followed in similar footsteps to the scholar John Wyclif who lived over a hundred years before me. He translated the Latin Bible into English for the first time. By the time I came along, I wanted even the ordinary people to find again the truth and power of the Word of God. By having the Bible written in language they could understand, it would help them to find a relationship with God through Jesus Christ.
Leader: So you didn't think the Bible was boring then, as some people say?
Tyndale: 'Who said the Bible is boring?' should not be your question, but 'Who has got a Bible that they can read for themselves?' When you actually read the Bible, you find it is far from boring.
Leader: So what did you do, then?
Tyndale: I set about writing a new translation, in English, but by going back to the original Hebrew and Greek texts. And I made this the object of my life's work. When someone said to me that God's laws were not important, I strongly disagreed. My desire was for everyone, down to the young boy pushing a plough, to know more of the Bible.
Leader: Surely, you could have got into big trouble?
Tyndale: Yes, the authorities didn't like the fact that my new translation sometimes challenged what they had been teaching for years. They wanted to keep control of the people and didn't want them reading the Bible for themselves and making up their own minds what God wanted. I knew the risk that I was taking because seven people had recently been killed for teaching their children the Lord's Prayer, the Ten Commandments and the Creed in English.
Leader: And this didn't put you off?
Tyndale: I soon realised that I could not safely stay in England if I was to complete my work, and so I moved to Germany. The copies of the New Testament, which I shipped to England, were eagerly bought and read by ordinary people. They would sit up all night reading it. Sadly, many copies were destroyed by some in authority who felt threatened by ordinary people having their own New Testament Bible.
Leader: It must have taken some 'expert engineering' (*children respond to today's title by standing to attention*) to ship the English New Testaments from Germany, and it is hard to believe that some church leaders would want to prevent people from reading them! So, did you continue?
Tyndale: I did, and by 1529 I had translated the first five books of the Old Testament as well, but it was lost in a shipwreck!
Leader: Oh, no! All that work! So, what did you do?
Tyndale: My friend, Miles Coverdale, helped me prepare a second manuscript, this time completing the first fourteen books of the Bible; up to the book of Second Chronicles.

Leader: Well done for persevering!

Tyndale: And, after my death, the king ordered that a copy of the Bible, that Coverdale and I had translated into English, be placed in every church in England. Also he encouraged everyone to read it. Now that was 'breaking new ground!'

Leader: But the 'breaking new ground', to give the common person the opportunity to read the Bible for himself, was clearly not easy for you. Thank you for talking with us.

Tyndale: Goodbye now, and keep up with your Bible reading. The Word of God is a treasure.

Leader: Goodbye. (*Closes phone*) Well, we certainly need to be grateful for 'groundbreaking' people, such as William Tyndale, who gave his life so that we may all read the Bible for ourselves.

Idea from, and for further reading: 70 *Great Christians Changing The World*, © 1992 Geoffrey Hanks and Christian Herald, Christian Focus Publications Ltd. ISBN 1 871676 80 0

Bible story: 'Expert Engineer Elijah'

This story outline has been tried and tested. Use it as a guide and adapt to suit your particular group and situation. Appropriate 'rocks' at key points in the story are suggested in brackets (see How to use Elijah's Altar).

TIPS OF THE TRADE

Three or four volunteers can practice the mime drama with the storyteller before the day. Use a large altar from the Creative Construction time as a prop, acting side on, or front on, to the audience, where possible.

Elijah was a prophet (someone who hears and speaks God's word to others) who came from Northern Israel and spoke God's word to the king and the nation of Israel. Elijah's name means 'the Lord is my God'.

(Rock 1: crown) He lived in a time when the king of Israel did many evil things in the sight of God, and many in the land worshipped the false god, Baal, and the false goddess, Asherah.

King Ahab married Jezebel who also worshipped Baal, and displeased the Lord God whom Elijah served.

(Rock 2: Jezebel) One day God gave a message to Elijah for King Ahab. God said there would be no more rain until he commanded.

(Rock 3: rain cloud and rain) (*Children put their hands out as if to feel the rain.*) God sent Elijah to a

small stream and provided bread and meat flown in by ravens each day and water to drink from the small stream.

(Rock 4: raven) Then the Lord God sent Elijah to a widow in Zarephath of Sidon, who lived with her young son, who gave him food and a place to stay.

(Rock 5: young boy) The widow only had a small amount of flour and oil but when she shared it with Elijah, something happened. Can anyone guess what happened next? (*Pause.*) God did a miracle by making more oil and flour for her to bake cakes and bread. Imagine that – her jar of flour and jug of oil didn't run out in a time when food was scarce! She had enough food during the years of the very bad drought for herself, her young son and Elijah.

(Rock 6: flour and jars of oil) (*Children pretend to be enjoying eating bread.*) Then, after three years, God commanded Elijah to go to King Ahab. He told Ahab to summon the people from all over Israel to Mount Carmel. The invitation was to include the 450 false prophets of Baal and 400 prophets of Asherah, who ate at Jezebel's table.

(Rock 7: Mount Carmel) Elijah, filled with boldness from God, challenged all the people to choose between Baal or the Lord God. He set a challenge for all to see! (*Several prepared team members could now come forward to mime the false prophets killing the bull and preparing their altar, as the speaker continues.*) The challenge was for the prophets of Baal to kill a bull, lay it on a prepared altar and call to their god (this is called offering a sacrifice). Elijah would do the same and call to the Lord God. The true God would answer by sending fire to burn up the sacrifice.

(Rock 8: Elijah) The people agreed and the prophets of Baal made their altar, killed their bull and laid the pieces of meat on the wood. They called to their god from morning till noon; they cut themselves; they danced; they shouted. (*Pause as actors wave arms frantically.*) They did all they could to arouse Baal's attention, but there was no response. (*Pause. Children to look shocked, surprised, some find it funny.*) Elijah called to them, 'Shout louder! Surely Baal is a god! Perhaps Baal is asleep or he is deep in thought or he is busy. Maybe he is travelling elsewhere!'

(Rock 9: Baal idol) (*Children to screw up their faces at the sight of such a false god.*) Then, from noon till the time for the evening sacrifice, they danced and shouted and cut themselves till their blood flowed. They shouted louder and louder on the mountain. (*Children to shake their heads in amazement at such behaviour and put hands over their ears. Pause.*) Nothing happened. They must have been exhausted and very embarrassed (and bloody)!

Elijah called the people to him, repaired the old altar of the Lord like an 'expert engineer' (*watch for children standing to attention in response to today's title*) and laid twelve stones, one for each tribe of Israel. He laid the pieces of bull on the dry wood, carefully arranged on the twelve stones. He dug a trench around the altar, and asked that four large jars of water be filled and poured over the offering and the wood.

(Rock 10: water jar) When they had poured the first four jars of water over the offering, he asked them to do it again, and then again! (*How many jars of water were poured over the offering?*) By now, hundreds of litres of water filled the trench and water dripped from the stones, the wood and the offering. Then he prayed out loud to the Lord God of Israel, 'Answer me, O Lord, answer me so these people will know that you, O Lord, are God...' (memory verse: 1 Kings 18:37a). Suddenly, fire fell (like lightning) and burnt up the offering, the stones, the wood, even the pools of water. Everything was burnt up! (*Children look open-mouthed.*)

(Rock 11: fire) When all the people saw how the Lord God (Elijah's God) answered, they all fell to the ground and cried, 'The Lord, he is God! The Lord - he is God!' (*Children to bow forwards shouting together, 'The Lord, he is God! The Lord – he is God!' Pause.*)

Elijah commanded that all the false prophets of Baal be seized and killed in the Kishon Valley. (*Those acting as false prophets can now be 'killed'. Pause.*) For so long Elijah felt he had been fighting against the tide. Now his faith was strengthened by the Lord God.

Elijah now climbed to the top of Mount Carmel and prayed to the Lord God to send rain. (*Children to put their hands together in prayer.*)

(Rock 12: Praying hands) It had not rained in Israel for three and a half years! Imagine that! The ground was brown and dusty; the streams had dried up; the grass had virtually disappeared; no doubt food was becoming scarce and living conditions were not good. (*Children to pretend that dust is getting in their eyes and that they are thirsty!*) Elijah bowed low and prayed with faith until rain came that day! Today we remember Elijah, a man God used in 'breaking new ground'. (*Children respond,* **'GROUNDBREAKERS!'**.)

How to use Elijah's Altar:

Twelve rock shapes are drawn, cut out and positioned with (stick on stick) hook 'Velcro' on the loop nylon presentation board on the easel/flip chart. Each rock will also need to have a tab of loop 'Velcro' on the front to receive the picture. This is designed to represent Elijah's large altar of the twelve tribes of Israel. Draw the twelve pictures to fit on the rocks (as indicated within the brackets in the story, or use words and simple line drawings). As the story is told, the pictures are stuck onto the appropriate rocks with stick on stick hook 'Velcro'. When the eleventh picture is added (the flames of fire), it looks like an altar on fire.

Your altar may look similar to this:

Additional song ideas:

'Be bold, be strong' SFK 6;
Blessed be the name of the Lord; EP 5
'I hear the sound of the army of the Lord' MP 273;
'This is the day' JP 255;
'We shall stand' MP 737;
'My lips shall praise you' S 369;
'Our God is so great (big)' S 420.
'In the presence of your people' SF 220

EXPERT ENGINEER ELIJAH DIGGING SHEET 1

Fill in the missing words:

'Answer _ _ _, O Lord, _ _ _, me,
so these people will know that you,
O _ _ _, are God...' 1 Kings chapter 18, verse 37a.

What differences can you see between these two altars?

A.

B.

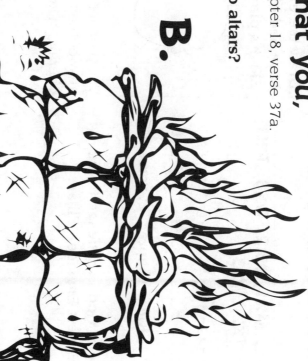

What's cooking?

If you can see six stones, how many are on the other side?

What do you understand about the Lord God?

Which altar did Elijah the 'Expert Engineer' build, A or B? ☐

Draw what was left after God sent the fire?

Full Name: _____

Age: _____ **Site Corner:** _____

DAY 3

Each different letter in the memory verse has been put in once for you. Fill in the missing letters the number of times shown below (for example, there are three missing letter 'A's two letter 'D's):

Ax3, Dx2, Ex8, Hx1, Lx4, Mx1, Nx2, Ox8, Px1, Rx4, Sx3, Tx2, Wx3

'A _ s _ _ r m _ , O L _ _ _ _ n _ w _ _ _ e,

_ _ t _ _ _ p _ _ _ _ i _ _ k _ _ _ _ h _ _ y _ u,

_ _ _ d _ , _ _ _ G _ _ _ .' 1 Kings chapter 18, verse 37a.

Draw something from the scene of God's challenge to the prophets of Baal, through his 'Expert Engineer' Elijah.

Full Name: _____

Age: _____ **Site Corner:** _____

Think of a newspaper headline for this event.

Draw the expressions that the prophets of Baal might have had on their faces when the Lord God answered Elijah's prayer with fire?

The prophets of Baal strongly believed that their god would answer their prayers and send fire down to burn up the offering. **Why didn't this happen?**

Elijah strongly believed that God would answer his prayer with fire and that is exactly what happened. **Why did this happen?**

What is the difference between believing in Baal and believing in the Lord God?

DARING DESIGNER HEZEKIAH

BLUEPRINT REFERENCE

2 CHRONICLES 29–32

Memory Verse 'May the Lord, who is good, pardon everyone who sets his heart on seeking God – the Lord...' (2 Chronicles 30:18b,19a)

AIMS

- To understand that the Lord God desires us to seek him with all our hearts.

- To understand that we are made in his image – to know him, to worship and serve him.

- To realise that we can talk to God about anything.

- To understand that he requires us to be holy as he is holy.

- To know that he is our protector – the one we can trust in all circumstances.

the plumb line

Why should we seek God?

The Bible teaches us that if we set our heart on seeking God, we will find him (Matthew 7:7,8). As we are made in his image, to come into a living relationship with God is the very purpose of life (John 17:3). We can know, talk to and listen to him. He promises to guide us through the Bible and by his Holy Spirit. God sees the big picture; we only see part of it. God loves us, knows and wants the best for us. If we seek him, he will give us wisdom and direction. If we 'seek first his kingdom and his righteousness' (Matthew 6:33), then all our other needs will be supplied.

Preparing Construction Site: Check that the Construction Site is set out correctly for the session.

Foremen's Fuel (25 minutes)

Hezekiah, when he became king, did not follow the evil ways of his father. He loved God's Word and sought God's ways for the people of Israel and Judah. He opened the temple of the Lord, had worship restored and encouraged the public reading of God's Word. He praised and trusted God in times of difficulty. George Müller (today's central drama character) prayed for the provision of homes and education for homeless children. He taught the children the ways of God. Pray that you will be able to share why you desire to worship God.

Open with a short prayer.

Bible reading: 2 Chronicles chapters 29:1–6,15–18, 20–31,35,36; 30:1,2,13–27; 31:1,2,20,21; 32:1–8,16–30. Share the reading from some of the selected passages.

Questions for the Site Manager to put to the Foremen:

- How did the Israelites worship God?

- Why does God require our worship?

- In what ways did Hezekiah seek God?

- In what situations have you had to seek God for wisdom or protection?

Ask the Foremen to identify the key points in the story, which should include:

- King Hezekiah was godly and led by example.

- The temple of God was opened and worship and religious festivals restored.

- Hezekiah trusted and called out to God when confronted by the King of Assyria and his army, and experienced God's protection.

- He organised the people to make weapons, repair the walls and build a water system for Jerusalem.

DAY 4

Fact File on George Müller:

Born in Prussia in 1905; baptised and confirmed in the Lutheran Church; while training to be a pastor, he confessed his sinful ways; he came to England, married and lived trusting God to provide for him; he realised his vision to open an orphanage in 1836, praying in the funds and caring for and educating the children in the ways of the Lord; delegated the running of the Homes to his son-in-law and travelled abroad to preach the gospel to the unconverted wherever he went; financially supported many missionaries like Hudson Taylor; funded one hundred schools; gave out four million tracts; distributed thousands of copies of the Scriptures and catered for 10,024 orphans; an outstanding example of a man of faith and prayer, he died in 1898. (See web site, details on page 3 to download Fact File on acetate.)

Brief testimony: A team member could share about a situation where they had to seek God for wisdom, protection or direction. (This could be shared in their Site Corner, if appropriate, during Creative Construction.)

Prayer: Allow time to pray together.

Preparing Site Corner: Make sure everything is ready for the activities at the Site Corners.

Tools For The Trade

ID: Construction Site Passes and Builders' Bands, or materials to make them.

Site Corner starter: Reference and materials to make the signs (see Welcome).

Music: Word acetates and music for **GROUNDBREAKERS!** and other action songs. Background audio tape.

Reconstruction: Costumes, props and scripts.

Bible story: Video episode 4, and/or artwork, notes and equipment for the retelling of the story. (See page 49 or **GROUNDBREAKERS!** web site for other visuals.)

Memory verse: Acetate or other prepared materials.

Digging sheets: Day 4, Bibles, coloured pencils, etc.

Creative Construction: Materials for craft activity previously chosen from the options under Take Your Pick

Refreshments: Cold drinks and biscuits.

Game: Appropriate equipment for optional game.

Welcome (Total 20 mins)

Registration

Have background audio tape playing quietly as Builders arrive.

TIPS OF THE TRADE

Draw the sign out on flat card. The first stage of the sign could have been prepared (shape, symbol and or word(s) to complete) beforehand.

Site Corner starter

Builders' Bands are reissued to Builders and new Builders' Bands issued to any new Builders. Make a construction sign together for your Site Corner, eg 'Men at work', 'Danger', 'Must wear hard hats' or design your own.

Site Meeting (Total 30 minutes)

Site Manager calls, 'Breaking new ground', and following the response, '**GROUNDBREAKERS!**' says, 'Down tools and assemble for site meeting.' Builders and Foremen assemble.

Builders' brief (3 minutes)

Remind Builders of dos and don'ts, fire exits, toilets, first aiders, etc. and highlight the **GROUNDBREAKERS!** postbox.

Songs (10 minutes)

Remind Builders of the **GROUNDBREAKERS!** chorus (with actions) and introduce all verses. See whether the children can sing it all through. Include other action songs (see page 50).

Bible story (10 minutes)

Episode 4 of the **GROUNDBREAKERS!** video, or retold Hezekiah story (see page 49). After using the video, check that the children have grasped the story, especially the way in which Hezekiah brought about a renewed worship of God. Make sure you have introduced the memory verse.

Reconstruction (7 minutes)

Ask the Builders to stand to attention when they hear today's title, 'Daring Designer', and not to forget to call out, '**GROUNDBREAKERS!**' if they hear the cue, 'Breaking new ground.'

Following the Reconstruction, the Site Manager says, 'Take up your tools' to disband the Site Meeting. Builders to return to Site Corners.

Take Up Your Tools (Total 60 minutes)

Digging (10–15 minutes)

Digging sheets for Day 4 and discussion of key points (see page 45).

Creative Construction (30 minutes)

Builders in each Site Corner embark on the craft activities previously chosen by their Foremen from Take Your Pick.

Take Your Pick

1 Large praise letters

As a team, make the 'praise letters' W O R S H I P G O D or C E L E B R A T E G O D. Prepare the letter shapes by cutting each one out of strong card approximately 45 cm

TIPS OF THE TRADE

Cutting out the letters carefully beforehand will save useful time during the activity.

long x 30 cm wide. During the activity, decorate with pieces of shiny coloured hologram paper (available in various colours with a self-adhesive back). Add coloured stickers, silver and gold, smiley faces, etc, for decoration. Each child makes at least one letter. During the presentation each child holds their letter to spell the words to the audience.

TRIED AND TESTED

Attractive 'Praise Bunting' will be suitable to hang up on display after GROUNDBREAKERS! along the inside wall of a building for several months.

2 Multicoloured 'Praise Bunting'

Make this to hang along the inside of the building. Use brightly coloured A4 paper (fluorescent is particularly attractive). Fold in half (A5). From each corner of the folded edge cut diagonally to the middle of the opposite (opening) edge. This gives a triangular shape when folded (parallelogram if opened). On one side of each triangle shape (with point downwards) write one word from the memory verse (until memory verse is complete) and leave some additional blank triangles. Prepare a length of string (coloured?), long enough to suspend all the triangles. There should be enough triangles for each child in the team, plus some blanks (the minimum would be the words in the memory verse). This should all be prepared before the activity. Each child has a folded triangle and using coloured stickers, gold and silver stars, washable marker pens, etc, decorates the triangles (they should have time to do more than one). When finished they should be hung on the length of string and located by the Foreman with two staples (use coloured paper clips if necessary). (See Digging sheet for younger children.)

3 Praise banner

This is made from an offcut of a plain shower curtain or other spare fabric. Suggested size is 90 cm x 60 cm. Stick (check glue is suitable) or stitch coloured felt, lettering and shapes in a unique praise design. The banner should be folded top and bottom and stitched, to allow for a dowelling rod to be inserted 100 cm in length (approximately). This should be prepared beforehand. On the top dowelling rod, coloured cord or string can be attached to allow the banner to hang.

4 King Hezekiah's crown

To be made and worn by the young children. Use coloured hologram card, measured and cut to the child's head size. Decorate with coloured stickers, scrunched tissue paper, cotton wool, etc. Coloured tassles can be made from crêpe paper and attached. When decorated, the crown is made to the child's head size and held together by wide masking tape on the inside (staples or pins are not recommended). The child's name can be written on the inside. When presenting, the children all boldly wear their crowns.

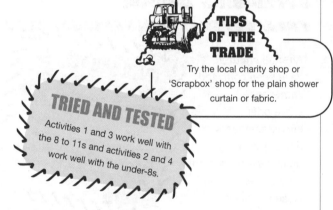

TIPS OF THE TRADE

Try the local charity shop or 'Scrapbox' shop for the plain shower curtain or fabric.

TRIED AND TESTED

Activities 1 and 3 work well with the 8 to 11s and activities 2 and 4 work well with the under-8s.

Refreshments

Site Clean-up! (3–5 minutes)

Site Manager calls 'Breaking new ground', then 'Down tools', and gives the Site Clean-up instructions.

Optional Game (5–10 minutes)

Indoor or outdoor game (if space and time permit).

DAY 4

Site Meeting (20 minutes)

Site Manager calls, 'Assemble for Site Meeting.' When all are assembled, Site Corners deliver their Building Presentations with a brief explanation by a Foreman using a microphone. The Site Manager highlights the title of the session; recaps on the memory verse to learn; mentions the competition sheet to enter (see web site); announces competition winners from Day 3; gives any notices; leads an optional song (if time allows); highlights items to take home (all activities are to be kept for the exhibition at the end of the week) and closes with a short prayer.

Builders return to their Site Corner, hand in Builders' Bands, collect their sheets and wait for the authorised adult to collect them.

Foremen's Debrief (5–10 minutes)

After all children have been collected, gather together to share brief encouragements or difficulties, plan practical arrangements for next session and close in prayer.

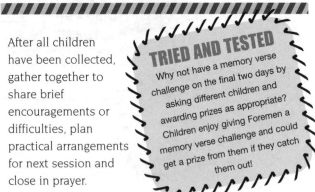

TRIED AND TESTED

Why not have a memory verse challenge on the final two days by asking different children and awarding prizes as appropriate? Children enjoy giving Foremen a memory verse challenge and could get a prize from them if they catch them out!

Reconstruction for Day 4
George Müller

Characters:
Narrator; George Müller; two boys (or two girls, or small youth/adults of the same sex); a baker; a milkman.

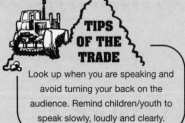

TIPS OF THE TRADE

Look up when you are speaking and avoid turning your back on the audience. Remind children/youth to speak slowly, loudly and clearly.

Props: Table and three chairs; fluorescent jacket/vest, hard hat and clipboard (with script) for narrator; black cassock and collar (see web site) for George Müller; white coat for baker; white and blue striped apron for milkman; plain grey trousers and white shirts for boys.

Scene: *The table is centre stage, one chair behind and one chair each end but set at an angle to slightly face the audience; Müller and children are off-stage to one side; baker and milkman off-stage to other side.*

Narrator: Today our Reconstruction from down the corridors of time takes us to an early children's home; known as an orphanage in those days. It is about a hundred and fifty years ago and the founder (the one who set up the orphanage), is a prayerful man called George Müller. You could say he was a 'daring designer' (*look out for children standing to attention in response to today's title*) of children's homes.

It is breakfast time one morning, but the food, and money to buy food, has all gone: there is nothing to eat. Müller has a home full of hungry boys and they are coming to breakfast as we join them...

Boy A: (*Entering with* Boy B *and approaching the breakfast table*) What do you think we are going to have for breakfast, then?

Boy B: The table is laid, but I can't see any food.

Boy A: I think we ate all that was left last night, and that wasn't much.

Boy B: Perhaps we'll go hungry. (*Rubs tummy.*)

Boy A: Shh; he's coming. (*Both boys hurry to stand quickly and quietly behind their respective chairs, leaving the middle chair for Müller.*)

Müller: Boys. (*The boys nod respectfully*) It is always good to talk to our Heavenly Father; let's pray. (*Children bow their heads and put hands together and Müller closes his eyes.*) Dear Father, we thank you for what you are going to give us to eat. Amen.

Boys: Amen. (*Boys look at each other, puzzled, shrugging shoulders, etc. Müller then sits down and the puzzled children curiously take their seats too.*)

Narrator: There is a knock at the door. (*Baker enters at side and knocks on imaginary door.*) 'KNOCK, KNOCK.' It is the local baker with a large tray of freshly-baked bread and Müller gets up and opens the door.

Baker: Good morning, sir. The Lord told me during the night to bake extra bread because it is needed. (*Hands Müller a large imaginary tray of bread.*)

Müller: (*Gratefully receives the bread as the children look on in amazement.*) Thank you, good man; the Lord has provided through you. (*Puts bread on the table to eager delight of children, and baker exits.*)

Narrator: Just as Müller sits down there is, almost immediately, another knock at the door. 'KNOCK, KNOCK.' Again, Müller goes to the door as the children watch. This time, it is the milkman with a churn of milk.

Milkman: Excuse me, but my milk cart has broken down...

Narrator: (*Interrupts quickly*) No milk floats or supermarket cartons in those days!

Milkman: Please could you use some of this milk for me (*hands Müller an imaginary churn which Müller receives* gratefully – remember it would be rather heavy). Then I can carry out the repairs to my cart.

Müller: Thank you, kind sir. The Lord is faithful: he hears and answers our prayers. (*Milkman exits as Müller brings the milk to the table to the thrill of the children, and sits down.*) Will you pass me the jug, son? (*Looks at Boy A.*)

Boy A: (*Passes jug*) Yes, sir.

Müller: (*Removing imaginary lid from churn, he dips in the jug and then pours milk out to each of them.*) This will be delicious.

Boys: Now we can have our breakfast! (*Enthusiastically getting ready to eat.*)

Müller: (*Raises hand*) Let us give thanks first. (*All bow heads to pray and freeze position until narrator has finished.*)

Narrator: Before the 'breaking new ground' could happen, there was much humble and private prayer by this man. He prayed in faith to the Lord for many needs without telling others. He lived by faith in this way and was never in debt, caring for over 10,000 children in his children's homes during his lifetime. Thank you for your attention to today's Reconstruction. (*All exit.*)

For further reading: 70 Great Christians Changing The World, © 1992 Geoffrey Hanks and Christian Herald, Christian Focus Publications Ltd. ISBN 1 871676 80 0

Bible story:
'Daring Designer Hezekiah'

////////////////////////////////////

This story outline has been tried and tested. Use it as a guide and adapt to suit your particular gifts, group and situation. Appropriate pictures at key points in the story are suggested in brackets (see How to use Hezekiah's Tunnel).

(Picture 1: crown with 25 on it) Hezekiah became king (in the year 715 BC) when he was just 25 years old. He lived in a way that pleased the Lord God, unlike his father, Ahaz. He reigned as king for twenty-nine years and removed all the horrible things in the temple, which had displeased God. He had the temple repaired and cleaned; the priests were properly trained; the people began to worship the Lord again.

TRIED AND TESTED
Have someone not involved, to watch for children standing to attention in response to today's title. When children call out the 'GROUNDBREAKERS!' response, be ready to repeat the sentence.

(Picture 2: the word 'worship') He invited (*children can beckon with one hand to each other to come*) all the people, from all the tribes of Israel and Judah, to come to Jerusalem to celebrate the special feast called the Passover. Some people thought this idea was silly (*children to pull faces and shake heads and pretend to mock and laugh*) but others came to the celebration where there were thousands of people.

(Picture 3: happy face) There was singing and great rejoicing and God heard the prayers of his people in Israel. Hezekiah prayed, 'May the Lord, who is good, pardon everyone who sets his heart on seeking God – the Lord...' (memory verse: 2 Chronicles 30:18b,19a.) God forgave the people for all the wrong they had done. Not since the days of King Solomon had there been any celebrations like this in Israel.

(Picture 4: King Hezekiah) Hezekiah encouraged the Israelite people to follow the ways God wanted. They were not to follow idols but they were to worship the Lord God. Hezekiah encouraged the people to give God some of their possessions, by giving to the priests and the Levites who worked in the temple, so that they could concentrate on understanding the law and serving the Lord. The Israelite people smashed down the idols (like the Asherah poles), the high places and sacred stones of worship to false gods.

(Picture 5: scroll of the word of God) Hezekiah was faithful in obeying, wholeheartedly, the commands of the Lord his God. Things went well, as God blessed him and the people. (*Children to hold up one of their thumbs, with a smile and a nod.*)

During his reign he became ill (in about 702 BC) and would have died, but he wept and prayed (*children pretend to pray and cry*) to the Lord God.

(Picture 6: sad face) God made Hezekiah better within a short time and said, 'I will deliver you and this city from the King of Assyria.'

Almost a year later, the King of Assyria, Sennacherib, was attacking Israel and capturing many of the people and the cities. He sent many of the richer people to Assyria and planned to attack and capture Jerusalem. He was a very proud king who thought he could win because of his own strength and power. (*Children to look puffed up, proud, boastful, some could flex their muscles.*)

Hezekiah organised his people to defend Jerusalem. He was very clever and a 'daring designer' (*watch out for children standing to attention in response to today's title*) who built a tunnel to provide a water supply for all of Jerusalem.

(Picture 7: water) In those days, you see, water had to be fetched from a spring or a river outside the city. If the city was surrounded by an enemy army, the people would not be able to get out to fetch water. (*Ask the children what happens when people do not have water?*) He organised two groups of men with axes to tunnel their way through rock and stones.

DAY 4

(Picture 8: axe) They met after 1750 feet (approximately 540 metres) of tunnelling, no doubt with sore hands and looking very grubby! (*Point to the tunnel and explain it's a cross section through.*) He also organised the building of weapons and shields so that the people could protect their city.

(Picture 9: weapons and shield) The field commander of the Assyrian army boasted about his strength. He asked whether any god had been able to protect its people from the mighty king of Assyria and how then could the Lord save Jerusalem? Hezekiah had told all the people not to say or do anything. (*Children all put their forefinger over their mouth and say 'ssshh'.*) When the message came to Hezekiah, he went into the temple, tore his clothes, put on sackcloth and prayed; he knew it was good to talk to the Lord God.

(Picture 10: praying hands) God sent a message through Isaiah the prophet, and told Hezekiah he would send the king of Assyria away to his own country.

(Picture 11: Isaiah) Soon afterwards Sennacherib, the king of Assyria, received bad news and he decided to leave in a hurry with his large army. As he left, he sent another nasty message full of rudeness to God (*children to look puffed up, arrogant, proud, boastful*), 'Surely you have heard what the kings of Assyria have done to all the countries around them, destroying them completely? What makes you think that you will be safe?' Hezekiah again went to the temple with this new letter and prayed to God. The Lord God spoke to Hezekiah through a message given to Isaiah the prophet: 'He will not enter this city or shoot any arrows here. I will defend this city and save it.'

(Picture 12: angel's hand pointing) Then the angel of the Lord went out and killed 185,000 men in the Assyrian army! When the rest woke up in the morning there were lots of dead bodies all around them! (*Children to look shocked, open-mouthed.*) The king of Assyria packed his bags and went home.

Hezekiah was literally able to 'break new ground' (*Pause. Children respond, 'GROUNDBREAKERS!'*) when he designed the construction of the tunnel to supply water for Jerusalem (which can still be seen today!). Hezekiah had restored the temple and encouraged worship to the Lord God in Israel. He knew how to praise and give thanks to God. He knew that the best thing to do was to seek God when things were difficult. He trusted in the Lord God when facing death through sickness and God added another fifteen years to his life. He also trusted God when facing the enemy, the King of Assyria, and God have him the victory. He was a 'daring designer' (*watch out for children standing to attention in response to today's title*), a faithful king and a remarkable 'Groundbreaker!'

How to use Hezekiah's Tunnel:

To create the impression of a cross section through Hezekiah's tunnel, 'Velcro' tunnel edges top and bottom of the loop-nylon presentation board, placed on an easel/flip chart. Draw (or write the words for) ten to twelve visuals as indicated within the brackets in the story. They are placed into position using stick on stick 'Velcro' within the edges of the tunnel.

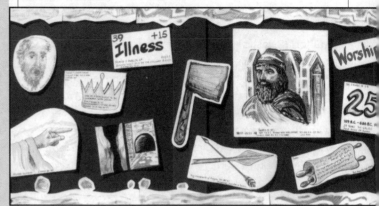

These visuals are an example of Hezakiah's tunnel, added to the tunnel by the storyteller (or Builders and Foremen) at the appropriate points in the story. Highlight Hezekiah's tunnel achievement, which can still be seen in Israel today. It is advisable to practice your presentation before going public. (The happy and sad faces can be cleverly drawn as the same face and just turned upside down to reveal the other expression, see diagram.)

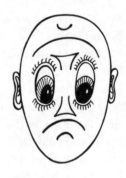

Additional song ideas:

'I hear the sound of the army of the Lord' JP 100;
'Lord, you put a tongue in my mouth' KS 243;
'I'm gonna thank the Lord' SFK 88;
'Blessed be the name of the Lord'; EP 5;
'I may never march in the infantry' JP 101;
'Hallelu, hallelu' JP 67.

DARING DESIGNER HEZEKIAH DIGGING SHEET I

Draw or write your idea of something that is really worth celebrating.

The words of the memory verse are jumbled. Can you untangle the streamers and write the verse in the bricks of the tunnel wall, below?

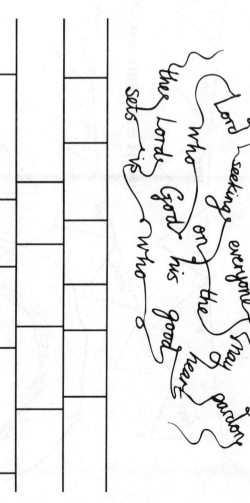

> Lord
> seeking
> everyone
> may
> pardon
> who
> on
> the
> heart
> thee
> Lords
> God
> his
> good
> sets
> is
> who

2 Chronicles chapter 30, verses 18b and 19a.

Do you want Jesus to be part of your celebrations?

Yes	Sometimes	No

Name and draw something with a daring design.

God designed us and wants us to worship him.

How does that make you feel?

Full Name: _____

Age: _____   Site Corner: _____

DARING DESIGNER HEZEKIAH DIGGING SHEET 2

DAY 4

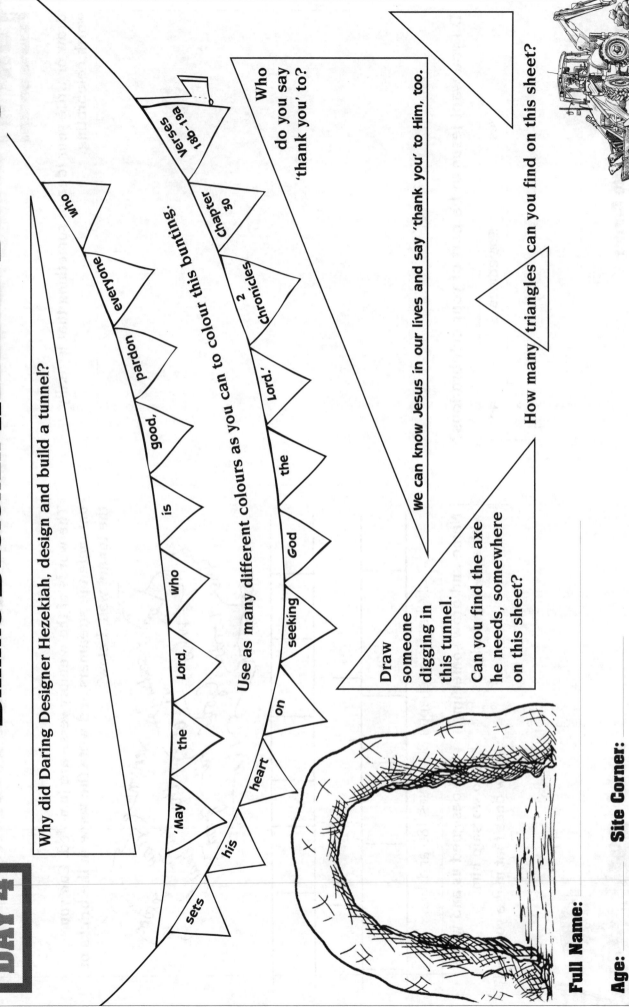

Why did Daring Designer Hezekiah, design and build a tunnel?

'May the Lord, who is good, pardon everyone who sets his heart on seeking God the Lord.'

2 Chronicles Chapter 30 Verses 18b–19a

Use as many different colours as you can to colour this bunting.

Who do you say 'thank you' to?

We can know Jesus in our lives and say 'thank you' to Him, too.

Draw someone digging in this tunnel.

Can you find the axe he needs, somewhere on this sheet?

How many triangles can you find on this sheet?

Full Name:

Age:

Site Corner:

JESUS THE CORNERSTONE

BLUEPRINT REFERENCE

LUKE AND JOHN,
especially **LUKE 5:17–26;**
JOHN 14:6; 19:17–30; 20:1–10.

Memory Verse

Jesus said, 'I am the way and the truth and the life. No-one comes to the Father except through me.' (John 14:6)

AIMS

- To begin to understand that Jesus is God and, because of his love for us, came to earth, 2000 years ago. He was born as a baby and lived the perfect life on earth.

- To realise how much he shocked and surprised people when he healed the sick, forgave people's sins and offered eternal life.

- To explain that despite his perfect life (and because of it), he was put to death on a cross (as the only acceptable sacrifice to the Holy God), but he was raised to life again. He died in our place but now he is alive and we can know him as our Saviour and special friend.

- Only with Jesus as the 'cornerstone' of our lives, can we be acceptable to God.

the plumb line

Why did Jesus come?

When God created the earth and humankind, he gave people free will to obey or disobey him. Adam and Eve disobeyed God and creation ceased to be perfect. God cannot tolerate disobedience or sin. Adam and Eve's relationship with God was marred. God, however, loved his creation and had a plan of salvation. He sent his only Son, Jesus, into this fallen world. Jesus came and demonstrated his love through words and actions, and ultimately by dying on a cross in our place. Jesus paid the price, which only he could do, because he was perfect. He took our sin on himself. God raised his Son to life. Jesus, who now sits at the right hand of his Father in glory, has sent his Holy Spirit to help us live God's way.

Preparing Construction Site:

Check that the Construction Site is set out correctly for the session.

Foremen's Fuel (25 minutes)

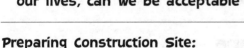

Jesus' miracles, healings, words and actions challenged people wherever he went. Josiah Spiers (today's central drama character) worked all his life to speak biblical truths to children. He went on to pioneer children's ministry in England, by setting up the Children's Special Service Mission and the beach mission ministry

Open with a short prayer.

Bible reading: Luke 2:1–11; 5:17–26; John 1:1–14; 3:16; 14:6; 18:28–38;19:17–30; 20:1–10.
Several team members read selected passages from the above.

Questions for the Site Manager to put to the Foremen:

- How do we know Jesus is God?

- How could God allow his only Son to be crucified?

- Why is Jesus the only way to God?

DAY 5

Ask the Foremen to identify the key points in the story, which should include the following:

- The Word was with God from the very beginning, became flesh and came to earth.
- Jesus healed people and challenged the religious authorities.
- Jesus taught people the right way to live. He claimed to be the only way to God the Father.
- Jesus was falsely accused, tried and murdered.
- On the third day, Jesus was raised to life.

Fact File on Josiah Spiers:

Born in the mid 1800s; concerned that children should hear the Word of God in a way they could understand; impressed by a leader of a service for children in London; on holiday in Llandudno joined children on the beach and, with them, wrote a text in the sand and told them a Bible story; returned each day of his holiday, thus the first beach mission was born; resigned his job and gave the rest of his life, without pay, to the work of Children's Special Service Mission (CSSM); described as 'a prince of speakers to children', his message focused on the love of God. Today, Scripture Union (formerly CSSM) has autonomous movements in over 130 countries, producing Bible notes and publications for all ages, running camps, beach missions, training and family events and working in schools. (See web site details on page 3 to download Fact File on acetate.)

Brief testimony: A team member could share about their relationship with God through Jesus. This could be shared in their Site Corner, if appropriate, during Creative Construction.

Prayer: Allow time to pray together.

Spiritual Response: Following all that they have heard about God during **GROUNDBREAKERS!**, today the Builders will learn that they can come to God through Jesus. Some Builders may be ready to make a sincere spiritual response to Jesus today. Some may want to pray, commit their lives to God and make Jesus their Saviour and special friend. People make a series of genuine faith responses to Jesus during their lifetime and this often begins in childhood. Some children may be making a recommitment, or asking for prayer for a particular need or situation.

Foremen need to be prepared for some children to make responses today. During the 'Digging' time, Foremen should invite any children in their Site Corner to come and talk with them, if they would like to pray a prayer of response to Jesus, at whatever level is appropriate. (Refer back to page 8.)

Preparing Site Corner:

Make sure everything is ready for the activities at the Site Corners.

TIPS OF THE TRADE

Remember never to pressurise children to make a response to Jesus. Invite them to come and tell you if they are ready.

There is a prayer response card (see page 26), that the child fills in with their Foreman. This can be given to the child and shown to the parent when collecting their child. This will help to explain that the child has responded to God in prayer. This may be an appropriate time to enquire whether the child has a suitable Bible and, if not, whether the parents would be happy for their child to be given one from the church.

Tools for the Trade

ID: Construction Site Passes and Builders' Bands, or materials to make them.

Site Corner starter: Materials to make miniature scaffolding (see Welcome below).

Music: Word acetates and music for **GROUNDBREAKERS!** and other action songs. Background audio tape.

Reconstruction: Costumes, props and scripts.

Bible story: Video episode 5, and/or artwork, notes and equipment for the retelling of the story (see page 57 or **GROUNDBREAKERS!** web site for other visuals).

Memory verse: Acetate or other prepared materials.

Digging sheets: Day 5, Bibles, coloured pencils, etc.

Creative Construction: Materials for the craft activity, chosen from the options under Take Your Pick.

Refreshments: Cold drink and biscuits.

Welcome (Total 20 minutes)

Registration

Have background audio tape playing quietly as Builders arrive.

Site Corner starter

Builders' Bands are reissued to Builders and new Builders' Bands given to any new Builders. Builders work together to design and make miniature scaffolding (using drinking straws or small, empty, sweet tubes, lolly sticks and thin string or narrow masking tape) to display in their Site Corner. Discuss why and how scaffolding is used.

Site Meeting (Total 30 minutes)

Site Manager calls, 'Breaking new ground', and following the response, '**GROUNDBREAKERS!**' says, 'Down tools and assemble for Site Meeting.' Builders and Foremen assemble.

Builders' brief (3 minutes)

Remind Builders of dos and don'ts, etc and highlight the **GROUNDBREAKERS!** postbox.

Songs (10 minutes)

Sing the full **GROUNDBREAKERS!** song (with actions). Include other action songs (see page 59).

Bible story (10 minutes)

Episode 5 of the **GROUNDBREAKERS!** video, or retold Bible story (see page 57). If you use the video, check that children have grasped the story and the idea that Jesus is the one way to know God. Make sure you introduce the memory verse.

Reconstruction (7 minutes)

Ask the Builders to stand to attention when they hear today's title, 'The Cornerstone' and not to forget to call out, '**GROUNDBREAKERS!**' if they hear the cue, 'Breaking new ground.'

Following the Reconstruction, the Site Manager says, 'Take up your tools', to disband the Site Meeting and Builders return to Site Corners.

Take Up Your Tools (Total 60 minutes)

Digging (10-15 minutes)

Digging sheets for Day 5 and discussion of key points (see page 54).

Creative Construction (30 minutes)

Builders in each Site Corner embark on the craft activity previously chosen, by their Foremen, from Take Your Pick.

Take Your Pick

1 Stained-glass window

A window of the cross and empty tomb can be made, using coloured tissue paper (or acetate coloured with non permanent OHP pens) and thick black A4 card, (see diagram on page 58). Make a few templates for the older children and for younger ones cut out the frames ready for them. Allow one frame for each child.

2 A cross

In two dimensions, this can be made of thick card, painted as rugged wood, with the children adding the labels of wrong things they have done, using thin dull-coloured card. These 'sin' labels can be irregularly cut out (or torn) and made to look ugly. In three dimensions, the cross can be made out of wood (prepared beforehand) with the 'sin' labels on thick card, tacked to the cross. The cross needs to have a firm base to support it.

3 A signpost

A large, team 3D signpost made out of a tube with slits cut to insert coloured card sign arrows. The stem of the signpost is to be supported by a weighted base. Sign arrows (of the wrong ways to go in life, eg greed, selfishness) are inserted and taped at different angles to the stem (don't forget one arrow to point to 'Jesus, the only way'). Signposts to be 90 cms or more in height.

4 2D signpost

Individual versions can be made on thick card (suggested size 10 cm x 21 cm). The signposts should be drawn and photocopied on pastel-coloured photocopier card. During the activity, these signposts are cut out and stuck onto a different coloured piece of card (10 cm x 21 cm). After discussion, as a team, about the wrong ways to live, Foremen write down the words suggested (in large lower case letters) for the children to copy. Don't forget that the arrow at the top is clearly for 'Jesus the only way'. When complete, the signposts could be covered in clear self-adhesive film and used as bookmarks. (See 8-11s' Digging sheet for example.)

5 The Cornerstone arch

This can be made in three dimensions, out of self-drying clay (or saltdough/playdough) on a hardboard base. Pieces of the arch are made and shaped (using clay modelling tools), into block shapes, and with wedge shapes for the top of the arch. These are built together, working from the base upwards, on both pillars of the arch. The final building stone that holds all the stones of the arch in place, is the cornerstone. These will all need to be allowed to dry in a safe place afterwards. (See the Digging sheet for example.)

> **TIPS OF THE TRADE**
>
> During the 'Creative Construction', Foremen should be ready to answer any questions that arise from the teaching of the day on the life of Jesus. If a child, or group of children, are ready to make a prayerful response but it is the middle of the activity, an Assistant Foreman can escort the child to the Site Manager, or to sit in a designated prayer area in the main hall, where someone will be ready to listen, pray and discuss issues with the children.

> **TRIED AND TESTED**
>
> Activities 1, 2, 3, 5 and 6 are more suitable for the 8 to 11s and activities 1, 4, 5 and 6 work well with the under-8s.

6 The maze game

This can be made using card partitions, tubes, etc in a cardboard box and illustrates the theme of going one way. Teams are encouraged to design their own game that allows a ball to go only one way through the maze. The suggested minimum dimensions of the cardboard box are 30 cm x 40 cm base x 10 cm height.

Refreshments

Site Clean-up! (3-5 minutes)

Site Manager calls, 'Breaking new ground', and then 'Down tools', and gives the Site Clean-up instructions. Quick clean-up before presentations.

Site Meeting (20 minutes)

Site Manager calls, 'Assemble for Site Meeting.' When all are assembled, Site Corners deliver their Building Presentations with a brief explanation by a Foreman using a microphone. The Site Manager highlights the title of the session; recaps on the memory verse to learn; announces the competition winners for Day 4; gives any notices (advertising the family events and services following on from **GROUNDBREAKERS!** and the exhibition for all parents and families); reminds about items to take home; finishes with the **GROUNDBREAKERS!** song and a short prayer.

Builders return to their Site Corners, hand in Builders' Bands, collect their sheets and any invitations to follow-up events, say 'Goodbye' to their Foremen and helpers and wait for the authorised adult to collect them.

Foremen's Debrief (10 minutes)

After all children have been collected, meet together to share encouragements or difficulties and close in prayer. Discuss clearing-up operation and the setting up of the **GROUNDBREAKERS!** exhibition, and immediate follow-up events. Allocate jobs.

Site Clean-up: (30 minutes plus)

Be prepared for a late break but put the kettle on!

Reconstruction for Day 5: Josiah Spiers

Characters: Narrator; Josiah Spiers; boy (youth/small adult); girl (youth/small adult); shopkeeper.

Props: Fluorescent jacket/vest, hard hat and clipboard (with script) for narrator; hat and jacket for Josiah Spiers (Victorian style); newspaper with script for Josiah (optional); long shorts (Victorian style) for boy with bare feet; dress (Victorian style) for girl with bare feet; white coat for shopkeeper; ball of string; 'dolly' wooden clothes pegs; large plastic (safe) spade.

Scene: *A raised platform/stage with steps down would be ideal at the back of this set (as promenade and steps to beach). The Narrator is standing at the opposite end of the stage to the steps; children are sitting motionless, about centre stage with the spade. Spiers is off-stage (preferably behind 'promenade'). The shopkeeper is off-stage at 'end' of promenade with string and pegs behind him/her.*

Narrator: We find ourselves on the coast in North Wales, for today's Reconstruction. It is 26 August 1868, and a lovely day at the relatively new seaside resort of Llandudno. (*Children quietly 'come to life' and act out making sandcastles with their hands - not moving around or saying anything.*) Josiah Spiers is visiting the area, as are many of the well-off families. It is a fact that children from richer families were less likely to go to Sunday School than those from poorer ones. What was Sunday School like, you may ask? Well, it was usually quite strict and you needed to be good at learning lots of passages from the Bible by heart. Children would have been expected to attend church services and had to sit upright (*pause, children immediately sit upright*), still (*pause, children sit very still*), but most of all silent (*pause, children put finger to lips - no smiling*).
(*Enter Spiers taking a stroll along the promenade, enjoying the warm weather and thinking - he could raise finger, nod, smile to himself, etc.*) Anyway, let's get back to this sunny day. (*Children visibly relax and start to play again on the imaginary beach.*) As Josiah walked along, he thought about things that had happened in the past year. Last year, in 1867, Josiah Spiers had taken a group of children to a service where the person leading had asked the children simple questions, told Bible stories and sung hymns and songs with tunes that the adults didn't know! This had been most unusual.

Spiers: (*Smiling to himself*) Just look at those children down there on the sand (*children start acting, collecting pebbles and seaweed and pretend to make a garden with them - so move around a little*). It looks as though they are making a garden out of pebbles and seaweed. (*He scratches his head as he has an idea.*) Do you know, those children could be writing a Bible text on the sand... I'll just go and buy some string and some pegs and then I will go down on the beach to join them. (*He walks away to get the items and goes to the shopkeeper along the promenade. Addresses the shopkeeper*) Please may I have some string and some pegs?

Shopkeeper: Certainly, sir. Just one moment. (*He turns to get them and hands them to him.*) Here you are.

Spiers: Thank you. (*Handing him/her some coins from his pocket.*)

Shopkeeper: Thank you. And I'm sure your washing will dry in no time, sir. Goodbye.

Spiers: (*Hesitates*) Er? Goodbye. (*Turns to leave, shows puzzled expression to audience and scratches his head.*) Washing?! (*Looks at string and pegs and realises the connection.*) Oh, yes! (*Slight chuckle. Returns along the promenade to the steps.*) This is the way down to the beach. (*He goes down the steps to the children who look up as he approaches and speaks to them.*) Who'll help me write a text – a few words – in the sand?

Children: (*Jumping up, excitedly*) I will! I will!

Spiers: Collect some white pebbles then, while I use these pegs and this string to make straight lines. (*He does this as the children run back and forth with pebbles.*) Now, may I borrow your spade to mark out the letters for 'God is Love'?

Boy: Yes, sir (*hands Josiah his spade and watches him as he marks out the letters while the girl continues to gather pebbles*).

Spiers: (*Spells out*) G O D I S L O V E. There now, can you fill in the letters with the white stones?

Children: Yes! Yes! (*Eagerly do it until they have finished.*)

Boy: (*Pointing to one of the imaginary letters*) There's a stone missing here.

Girl: (*Adds another imaginary stone*) Will this do as 'the cornerstone'? (*Watch for children standing to attention in response to today's title.*)

Spiers: That will be fine. Well done. Good. (*Nods approvingly.*) God is love. (*Admiring their work with hands on hips.*)

Boy: What shall we do next?

Spiers: Shall I tell you a story?

Children: (*Jumping up and down with excitement*) Oh yes! A story, a story!

Spiers: Well, sit down everyone and I will begin... (*The children sit down and Spiers mimes telling a story, using gestures and facial expression as the narrator speaks again.*)

Narrator: Let's leave them at that point, having the very first story at the very first beach mission. Quite a crowd had gathered by this time and each day Josiah Spiers went down onto the beach to teach the children in this way. This was a new thing; he was certainly 'breaking new ground' (and by that I don't just mean digging in the sand!). Well, that just about concludes our series of Reconstructions for this **'GROUNDBREAKERS!'**. Thank you for your time. (*All exit.*)

For further reading: *A Tale of Two Visions: The story of Scripture Union Worldwide* by Michael Hews, Scripture Union Publishing, © 2000.

Bible story: 'Jesus The Cornerstone'

////////////////////////////////////

Adapt this material to suit your particular gifts, group and situation. See How to use Jesus the Cornerstone.

TRIED AND TESTED

This story outline uses the building principle of the 'Cornerstone' to help explain and illustrate some of the key miracles, teachings and life of Jesus.

Jesus is the ultimate **'GROUNDBREAKER'**. He broke ground in so many ways by the new things that he said and the different things that he did.

(Picture 1: Baby in straw = C for child) From the very beginning Jesus, who is God's Son, was with God. Two thousand years ago, Jesus came from heaven into this world - to show us God's love and teach us the way we should live - and was born in a smelly stable! Do you know where? (*Children to respond - 'Bethlehem'*) There were no television film crews, reporters or photographers when he was born as a **child**; just a few animals in the stable, his mother Mary, and Joseph.

(Picture 2: carpenter = O for ordinary things), Jesus learnt from his earthly father, Joseph, who was a carpenter, how to use tools to shape wood, to repair and make things for **ordinary** people in the hilly town of Nazareth where he lived. At about thirty years old, he was filled with God's power and given a special job, that only he could do. Within a short time, he walked on many **roads** to various places **(Picture 3: feet walking = R for road)**, 'breaking new ground' (*wait for children's response*) teaching people about God. Lots of people became excited because they hadn't heard powerful teaching like this from their religious teachers (Pharisees and Sadducees).

One man **(Picture 4: paralysed man = N for new legs)** who could not use his arms or legs to walk or even stand, was brought to Jesus on a stretcher. There was such a large crowd in and around the house where Jesus was, that his friends had to come up with an idea of how to get him inside to see Jesus. They decided to carry their friend up the outside steps of the house and make an opening in the flat tiled roof, big enough to lower their friend down in front of Jesus. Can you imagine what your parents would say if someone made a hole in your roof?! Well, Jesus looked up and saw, peering through the hole, the faces of the four friends. They had gone to such an effort to bring their friend to him, he praised their faith. He forgave the man for the wrong in his life *and* told him to pick up his bedding and walk! The man immediately began to wiggle his toes for the first time in his life! He started to move his feet and **new** legs and was amazed to find that he could

sit up without help from anyone else! (*Can you all wiggle your toes and fingers now? Just imagine what it felt like to do that for the first time.*) The man found he had new strength in his body and he stood upright and stretched. **Everyone** was amazed. **(Picture 5: amazed faces = E for everyone)** Very carefully he took his first step and then another and another and then, with new boldness, he found he was really walking! He was grinning from ear to ear and probably ran and skipped all the way home, full of joy, with legs as good as new. (*Children put on their widest smile.*) What a miracle! Can you imagine?!

This is only one of the many miracles that Jesus did (*Children all look amazed at each other.*) Jesus was 'breaking new ground' (*wait for children's response*) with people wherever he went. Jesus showed people how to love others, even their enemies! He taught them how to change their behaviour and to be honest. He was a perfect example of what God is like.

Jesus was popular with lots of people but others were angry with him. They did not like the things he said or the miracles he did. (*Children shake forefingers with angry expressions on their faces.*) Some were jealous, others felt threatened by Jesus, some even hated him and wanted him out of the way. Some of the leaders, religious teachers (Pharisees and Sadducees) and the important people, decided to kill him because he said he was the Son of God. (*Children pull shocked expressions.*)

One day they arrested him and said things about him that were not true. They took Jesus to the Roman Governor of Judea, Pilate. They wanted to have him crucified on a large wooden cross (the Roman way of killing) and Pilate eventually agreed to give them what they wanted. **(Picture 6: cross = E for Easter)** Around the world, churches remember that Jesus gave up his life and died on a cross at **Easter**. The Roman soldiers took Jesus and **nailed** his hands and feet to a large wooden cross. **(Picture 7: nails = N for nail)** Lots of people sneered and jeered at him when he was bleeding on the cross, but Jesus forgave them all, even Pilate and the Roman soldiers! Jesus died on a cross on a hill outside the city of Jerusalem, between two thieves.

It is a hard thing to understand why Jesus had to die but he did it because he loves us. He knew that this was the **only way** to come to God because we are not good enough on our own. **(Picture 8: one-way signpost = O for one way)** You see, God is holy and perfect and we are not. We do, say and think things that are wrong and which deserve to be punished. But Jesus, God's Son, who is perfect, came and took the punishment instead of us so that God could forgive us and we could be his friends. Jesus' death was the one way that we could get close to God and be forgiven.

(*Take the opportunity to further explain this in your Site Corners during the Digging time and Creative Construction.*)

Now, it would be a sad story if it ended there, wouldn't it? Let's see what happened after that though. Jesus' body was wrapped in cloths and buried in a newly cut **tomb** (or cave) in the rock. **(Picture 9: tomb = T for tomb)** On the Sunday, very early in the morning, some women, who were his friends, went to the tomb and found he was not there. The huge, heavy **stone** covering the entrance **(Picture 10: stone = S for stone)** had been moved away and there were some angels standing there in dazzling white. They told the women that Jesus had been brought back to life again just as he said he would. Other followers of Jesus, like Peter and John, ran to the tomb and found the empty burial cloths that had been wrapped around his body – Jesus was not there!

Later on that day, Jesus appeared to them and showed them the wounds in his hands and his side **(Picture 11: Jesus after his resurrection = R for resurrection/rise).** He ate with them and explained the reasons why he had to die and **rise** again. He had already told them that he is the truth and the only way to know God and go to heaven. They were all overjoyed and amazed. (*Children clap and cheer loudly and joyfully.*)

One day Jesus told the disciples, 'I am the way and the truth and the life. No one comes to the Father except through me' (memory verse: John 14:6). In the Bible, Jesus is sometimes called the 'Cornerstone' (*watch for children standing to attention in response to today's title. Position the final block [R = resurrection/ rise]*) to complete the archway that spells the word 'CORNERSTONE') The cornerstone can mean the foundation or finishing stone, that completes an arch or building and holds it all together. The cornerstone is the most important stone in a building - if it's not there, everything will fall apart. Jesus is the one who holds everyone in the church together. You can see that Jesus is the best 'Groundbreaker' of them all because he came to show us what God is like and he's the only true 'Cornerstone' (*watch for children standing to attention in response to today's title*) for our lives. You can ask Jesus to be your cornerstone – the foundation and finishing stone of your life. Now that would be truly groundbreaking!

How To Use
Jesus The Cornerstone:

Make a large archway out of card (see diagram). Cut it into 11 blocks and write the word 'CORNERSTONE' starting from the bottom left-hand column, as shown, ie one letter on each block. A doorway can be made out of card. (It acts as a helpful guide for positioning the blocks.) The blocks are put into position around the doorway during the story (one block added for each picture shown) by placing them on the loop-nylon board. Put stick on stick 'Velcro' on reverse side of each block. Start building from the lowest block on the left column (the first 5 blocks). Block 6 begins the right column with the Cornerstone block (letter 'R') being positioned last (see diagram for order of positioning blocks). Draw/design appropriate pictures or words, on card (as suggested in brackets). Do not forget to practice your presentation beforehand.

Additional song ideas:

'Great, great, brill, brill' SFK 48;
'I reach up high' KS 171;
'We want to see Jesus lifted high' SFK 181;
'King of Kings and Lord of Lords' MP 398;
'Come on and celebrate' SFK 15;
'Teach me to dance' KS 312;
'I'm gonna build my house on solid rock' SFK 86;
'Jesus is greater than the greatest heroes' KS 196;
'I'm special' SFK 162;
'Jesus, never never...' Kids Praise 2000, SH;
'I'm gonna click, click, click' KS 150 .

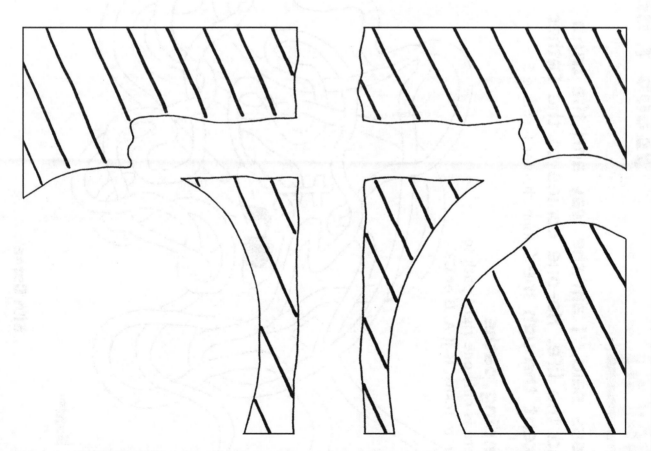

Enlarge to A4 size and cut out the shaded areas to make the template. Draw onto A4 black card and cut out as before.

JESUS THE CORNERSTONE DIGGING SHEET 1

Jesus said, 'I am the way and the truth and the life. No-one comes to the Father except through me.' John chapter 14, verse 6

Winding paths
There is only one right path to take to Jesus. Is it A, B or C?

A

B

C

Can you find the missing stone on the sheet?

How was Jesus a Groundbreaker?

How could you be a Groundbreaker?

Draw something that is living and something that is not alive?

Full Name:

Age:

Site Corner:

JESUS THE CORNERSTONE DIGGING SHEET 2

Fill in the missing gaps in the memory verse:

Jesus said, "I am the ___ and the ___ ___ and the ___. No-one comes to the F_ _ _ _ _ _ except through me."

John ch _ _ _ t _ r 14, v _ _ se 6

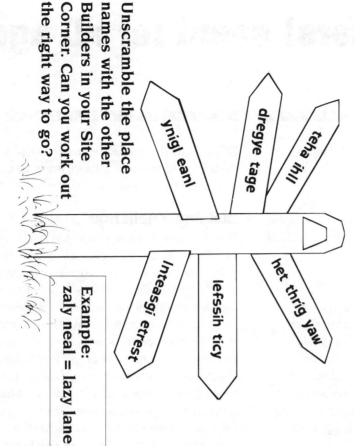

Unscramble the place names with the other Builders in your Site Corner. Can you work out the right way to go?

Example:
zaly neal = lazy lane

ynigl eanl

dregye tage

teha ihll

het thrig yaw

lefssih ticy

lnteasgi etrest

What happens to an arch without the cornerstone (capstone)?

Some things make us feel a bit wobbly and insecure in our lives: things like being ill or problems at school or in our families. Think of some things that make you feel like that.

How did Jesus make a difference to the man who couldn't walk?

How might Jesus be able to help you in your life if you asked him?

How was Jesus a Groundbreaker?

How could you be a Groundbreaker?

Can you circle the missing stone on the sheet?

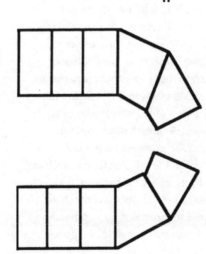

Full Name: _____

Age: _____ Site Corner: _____

Groundbreakers! event for all ages

(Approximately 3 hours)

If possible, set this up in the **GROUNDBREAKERS!** venue, decorated as a giant Construction Site. This event works especially well at the end of the week on the Saturday afternoon, complementing the all-age Sunday service. Or organise it fairly soon after **GROUNDBREAKERS!**. It is a useful means of maintaining contact with the children and building relationships with their families.

Building Stations (60 minutes)

Creative areas are set up around the main hall, on the building theme. The team will have prepared and set up their tables and resources earlier in the day. People are invited to have a go at as many of the building activities during the hour as they would like. These should cater for different ages: for example, playdough for younger children; building bricks; 'Duplo' brick houses; large soft toy building bricks (see if you can hire from a local toy library); book corner on building; designing 'Lego' construction vehicles; 'Jenga'; film canister tower building; playing-card buildings; model making; watercolour painting of construction sites; an educational construction tool area on supervised display; a competition to identify photographs of construction vehicles from unusual angles; a 'big art' picture using clothing and objects arranged on the floor to make a digger, a builder, a crane (this may only make sense when viewed from a higher position); other construction craft activities. These are just some suggestions. You will probably think of plenty more!

Refreshments (10 minutes)

Refreshments are served. Building stations are put away or moved to the edge.

Games (22 minutes)

Tangles Game (10 minutes): This involves children and adults. Tangles requires people to form mixed-age groups of ten or more around the room. The groups choose one adult to come aside and look away. The groups have a maximum of one minute whilst holding hands to form a circle and tangle themselves as much as they can without separating hands. Then they freeze in their position whilst their adult tries to untangle them by giving verbal instructions only.

Builders' Race (12 minutes): Teams sit down in semi-circles with paper and pencils. The games master will announce an object linked with the building theme, such as a boot, hard hat, spade, digger, drill, pick, hammer, Builder's Band, coin, keys, torch, ear protectors. Teams compete to find the real object (if available) or draw it on paper and place it on the designated chair in the middle of the room.

Different people in rotation have a go to enable everyone in the team to be involved. To finish, teams are challenged to make the most impressive building using their bodies.

Building Challenge (30 minutes)

Teams compete using junk packaging and boxes collected over the weeks. Give each team a large box full of junk, three pairs of large scissors (plus two pairs of children's scissors), a reel of parcel tape, a reel of sticky tape, three large marker pens and some string. Teams have to design a unique construction vehicle in the time given. On completion, each team nominates one person to present their construction and to attempt to persuade people to invest in it (up to 2 minutes per team). In the audience are four previously selected 'multimillionaires' looking to invest their millions. After all the teams have presented their designs, the millionaire judges are asked to vote. Award a **GROUNDBREAKERS!** prize. This is an ideal time for photography or video filming.

Construction Site Clear-up! (5 minutes)

What has Groundbreakers! all been about? (8 minutes)

Explain a little of what has gone on at the Construction Site during **GROUNDBREAKERS!**. Five craft pieces could be shown by the team, illustrating one key point of each story. Explain how Site Corners have learnt about teamwork, and how we can all fit into God's big building. Even though we make mistakes and are not perfect, God can forgive us. We are special to God. Sometimes we might face opposition as we follow God's ways and instructions. On a signal the **GROUNDBREAKERS!** drama begins (previously rehearsed).

Groundbreakers! Drama (7 minutes)

(see page 19)

Announcements (2 minutes)

Announce the all-age service details (if one is planned) for the following day. Thank everyone for their involvement this week, and all those responsible for the food arrangements, today. Guests are invited to the food area. Explain that there is no formal ending but people are free to go when ready.

Food (30 minutes)

The opportunity to mix and chat about the week, over food, telling the stories and highlights. Children can informally show their parents the craft work exhibition.

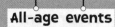

Parents and under-fives event and an all-age service

Parents and under-fives event

(Approximately 90 minutes)

A directed parents and under-fives event has enormous potential in the week of **GROUNDBREAKERS!**. Flyers distributed via the children attending the morning sessions will reach new children/families. Design the event on the building theme using appropriate activities as suggested for the all-age event. Toy tunnels can be placed on the floor. Soft play equipment may be hired from a Toy library/resource area. Building stations can be set up on tables which include playdough, building bricks, 'Duplo' brick houses, book corner on building, wall frieze using brick-shaped paint sponge prints.

Use action songs and rhymes. Include 'The wise man song', with actions (JP 252). Tell the story of the wise and foolish man who built on the rock and sand (Luke 6:46–49). Puppets are a very effective way of telling stories for young children. Alternatively, build two small, identical 'Duplo' houses, place one on a Duplo base and one on sand. Pour water around the two and see what happens!

This event has great potential in getting alongside parents and under-fives who may be outside the church/organisation. You may need to run a simultaneous programme to accommodate older brothers and sisters, in a separate venue, such as a video film, refreshments and games.

An all-age service (60–70 minutes)

If possible, use the **GROUNDBREAKERS!** venue, decorated with the building site resources on show. If in church, set up **GROUNDBREAKERS!** craft items around the building.

Welcome (2 minutes): Welcome everyone and mention the special week called **GROUNDBREAKERS!**, waiting for response.

Open with a prayer of thankfulness, thanking God for the special week that many children/adults have enjoyed.

Drama (7 minutes): Use the **GROUNDBREAKERS!** Drama (see page 19) if not used at the all-age event. Alternatively, present your favourite Reconstruction (drama).

Presentation 1 (6 minutes): Several items are displayed (different items from those shown at the all-age event) by several Foremen (with Builders), explaining what was made on Days 1 and 2 of **GROUNDBREAKERS!**.

Song (3 minutes): Sing the **GROUNDBREAKERS!** song, calling some Builders and Foremen to the front to help lead the actions.

Presentation 2 (6 minutes): Several items are displayed by several Foremen (with Builders), explaining what was made on Days 3 and 4.

Song (3 minutes): Sing a song that has been popular with the Builders during the week.

Prayer (3 minutes): A family involved in the week lead the church in prayers, ending with the Lord's Prayer displayed on an acetate on the OHP for all to see.

Presentation 3 (3 minutes): Several items are displayed by several Foremen (with Builders) explaining what was made on Day 5.

Songs (6 minutes): Use songs you have used during the **GROUNDBREAKERS!** week. Builders and Foremen can help lead the actions.

Groundbreakers! quiz (5 minutes): an opportunity to discover what the children have learnt! Ideas for presenting quizzes can be found in *The Quiz Resource Book* (SU).

Testimony (3 minutes): Opportunity to share any testimonies or encouragements by children or adults.

Dramatised reading (2 minutes): Luke 6:46–49, with children reading, while others mime the story. This will need a rehearsal!

Talk (10 minutes): Draw out the key points of the story. We are invited to hear what Jesus says and obey him – like the wise man. He did what was right. He set solid foundations for his house. Use the key points from the week to re-emphasise the best way to build our lives with Jesus as the Master Builder. Use some of the pictures of the Bible characters, craft items, and **GROUNDBREAKERS!** objects to illustrate the message (especially Jesus the Cornerstone).

A Foreman could share how he/she has chosen to build his/her life with Jesus as the foundation. (Make sure language and images are used which make sense to a child or unchurched adult. It can help to interview someone rather than give them five minutes to talk uninterrupted.)

Song (3 minutes): For I'm building a people of power (or something similar).

Notices and closing prayers (3 minutes): Invite all guests to stay to see the exhibition and refreshments. Finish with a big thank-you for all who have worked so hard to make **GROUNDBREAKERS!** such a special week.

Invite children to collect notices regarding the follow-up events planned by the church and to take home the exhibits they have made.

Order Form

To order any of the resources recommended in this book from **Mail Order**, complete this form.

The books should also be available from a local Christian bookshop.

ISBN	Title	Quantity	Price (each)	Price (each)

TOTAL COST OF GOODS	
Postage & packing	
Donation to Scripture Union	
TOTAL ENCLOSED	

When ordering, please include ISBN, title, quantity and price.

All titles subject to availability.

Prices subject to change without notice.

Ordering Information

Please complete the payment details below.

All orders must be accompanied by the appropriate payment.

Send this completed form to:

Scripture Union Mail Order

PO Box 5148

Milton Keynes MLD, MK2 2YX

Tel: 01908 856006 Fax: 01908 856020

Order Value	UK	Europe	Rest of World	
			Surface	Airmail
£6.00 & under	£1.25	£2.25	£2.25	£3.50
£6.01 – £14.99	£3.00	£3.50	£4.50	£6.00
£15.00 – £29.99	£4.00	£5.50	£7.50	£11.00
£30.00 & over	FREE	PRICE ON REQUEST		

Ordered by

Mrs/Mr/Miss/Ms/Rev ....

Address ....

....

....

....

Postcode ....

Daytime tel ....

(for any query about your order)

Delivery address (if different)

Mrs/Mr/Miss/Ms/Rev ....

Address ....

....

....

....

Postcode ....

Daytime tel ....

(for any query about your order)

Payment details

Method of Payment ☐ Cheque* ☐ Mastercard ☐ Visa ☐ Switch ☐ Postal order*

Credit card number: ☐☐☐☐ ☐☐☐☐ ☐☐☐☐ ☐☐☐☐   Expiry date: ☐☐☐☐

Switch card number: ☐☐☐☐☐☐☐☐☐☐☐☐☐☐☐☐☐☐   Expiry date: ☐☐☐☐

Issue number of switch card: ☐☐☐

Signature: ....   Date: ....

(necessary if payment by credit card)

*made payable to Scripture Union

Please print name which appears on credit card: ....

Please print the address the card is billed to, if different from above: ....

To be included on SU's supporters database and receive our quarterly SU News and other mailings please tick this box ☐   PBHCOl